The**facts**on**drugs**and**a**

Undruggedand**still**dancing

DebbieGoddard

Scripture Union, 207–209 Queensway, Bletchley, MK2 2EB, England.

© Debbie Goddard 1997

First published 1997

ISBN 1 85999 177 7

British Library Cataloguing-in-Publication Data.
A catalogue record for this book is available from the British Library.

Cover design by ie DESIGN.
Illustrations by Tony O'Donnell.

Printed and bound in Great Britain by Cox & Wyman Ltd, Reading.

CONTENTS

Intro 5

1 **Trippin'?** 7

2 **Crack the lies**
the facts on drugs and alcohol 15

3 **Speeding where?**
the road to addiction 48

4 **The high life**
true-life stories 56

5 **Sussed**
understanding who we are 71

6 **Under the influence**
handling the culture we live in 85

7 **Not to be sniffed at**
what the Bible says 98

8 **The real high life**
why we are here 107

9 **Sorted**
helping someone with a drug problem 114

Thank you

To all those who encouraged me and prayed while I was writing this. There are too many names to mention, but you know who you are. Please keep doing what you do, as I can't do my bit without you.

To my amazing friends whose stories are in this book. I know it was hard to write about painful memories. Thank you for making yourselves vulnerable so that others can learn from your experience.

To the youth groups in Haslemere and Birmingham who gave me such helpful comments on the first draft. Zoe Cowell, Esther Howkins, Helen Guyatt, Daniel Taylor, Chris Merritt, Vicky Pratt and Helen Barker, I hope you approve of the final result.

To Dick Durrant and Johnny Sertin for your encouragement and help.

To Dick and Meg for so generously letting me gatecrash your awning at Stoneleigh. If you hadn't, would I ever have written this?

INTRO

? What do drugs do to you?
? Is it wrong for me to drink when I'm under the age limit?
? How does God feel about me smoking?
? If someone offers me drugs, how can I say 'No' without feeling stupid?
? Isn't it okay for a Christian to take drugs now and then? Surely it's only wrong if you get addicted?

These are some of the questions I'm regularly asked by young people who are Christians or who are involved in church activities. Some are straightforward to answer, just needing factual information. Others are more complicated – they force us to think about things like what makes us tick, and how we can know what God feels about something that isn't spelt out in the Bible. The fact is that drugs are one of many things people may get into when they don't realise who they are and what they're here for. This means that we can't really separate these personal issues from the drugs issue, and it's the reason why I've included chapters on subjects that at first glance don't seem to have much to do with drugs. 'Just say "No"' isn't all there is to it!

This book is written mainly for those who want a Christian perspective on drug and alcohol use, and who aren't heavily involved in drugs. But I hope there is still something here that will make sense to those of you who haven't yet heard much about what being a Christian means, or who are well into drugs.

Five young people have written their stories, so that you can benefit from their 'true-life' experiences. I hope that between us we will cover what you want to know, help you work out how you want to live and, most of all, encourage you to go after God – the only source of all we're really looking for.

1 TRIPPIN'?

Rebecca

'If you carry on like this, you'll be addicted to heroin in ten years time,' the interviewing police sergeant threatened. It sounded ridiculous.

'No way,' I protested. 'It's only dope. I've no intention of ever doing anything else.' *Typical over-the-top adult response*, I thought. I was fifteen, and my boyfriend Mike and I had just been caught smoking a joint in the town car park. It was the first time I'd ever been in trouble and it was quite exciting!

The excitement didn't last long. The total humiliation of being strip-searched, and a few hours in a disgusting police cell with a dirty loo in the corner and a concrete shelf for a bed, changed my mood dramatically! I was terrified they might ring my parents. Now here I was, standing in front of an imposing-looking policeman, desperately hoping he would release me before my secret was discovered.

The shock of that incident soon faded and I carried on as before. It was only dope, I was only doing what many teenagers do, and I had no intention of taking it any further. The police in our little town probably told all young drug users that they would end up addicted to hard drugs. But on this occasion the sergeant was right.

For about a year I'd been starting to rebel against my upbringing. I'd asked Jesus into my life when I was eight, but by the time I was fourteen I didn't want to know anymore. I couldn't see the relevance of Christianity at school or in the world around me: boys, drinking and cigarettes were much more fun. I intended to give my life back to God on my deathbed so that I could still go to heaven, but in the meantime I would do all those other things that were so much more interesting.

My mother had been struggling with cancer throughout my life, and eventually died a month after my eighteenth birthday. I watched her suffering and couldn't understand how God could allow it to happen. I thought she was crazy, loving a God who was letting her die so slowly and painfully. Two months later I ran away from my grief by moving to London with my boyfriend. Once I'd left home, I smoked pot most of the time – a habit that was to continue for the next ten years. I also started using 'recreational' drugs, such as Speed, Acid and Mushrooms topped up with alcohol, 'for fun' at the weekends. I'd always wanted to work in the music industry and, to my delight, I got a job with a well-known record company. It seemed like I'd arrived! But, after the initial excitement, I felt really let down. I was meeting famous people, going to free gigs every weekend, being part of the 'in-scene', but it wasn't making me happy like I'd thought it would.

I became really excited by the idea of travelling and escaping from what had become dull monotony in

England. So when I was twenty-two John, my boyfriend at the time, and I set off for the Far East and Australia. Right from the start, it was a party. Everyone we knew and virtually everyone we met took drugs. On the surface, I was having a great time and going along with the crowd. Australia was beautiful and I loved travelling, but inside myself I was a mess. Although I covered it up, I was insecure and nervous about talking to people, and I thought nobody liked me. Looking back, I can see that they *did* like me – it was because I didn't know who I was that I was so nervous. I began to blame the mess inside myself on John and resent him for being around.

After a year in Australia, we set off back to England via Thailand. When we arrived home, I felt really depressed. Everyone's lives seemed so boring, and I craved some excitement. John and I split up, and I moved into a lovely flat in the countryside. I'd become interested in the environment while travelling, so I was thrilled when I got a job working for an international wildlife conservation charity – another dream come true! When my new job turned out to lack the excitement and meaning I craved, I started getting into the club scene, and went to party away every weekend in London. I used a lot of Ecstasy at this time and my health really deteriorated. At one point I was signed off work for three weeks because I was so run down. I was blind to what my drug use was doing to my body and mind, and thought my depression and ill-health were caused by the 'something' that was still missing in my life.

I started to search seriously. I ate as little as possible because I thought getting down to eight stone would mean instant happiness! I bought books on dreams and tried to analyse mine, thinking there was a great secret to be found this way. (I never found it!) I studied Buddhism for a new way to live, but I could never really get the hang of what it was all about. I tried to meditate, but on one occasion I had a terrifying experience – as I emptied my head of all thoughts, I felt as though a force of some kind was trying to control my mind. I have never meditated since!

One day I impulsively rang Mike, my ex-boyfriend. By now he was a registered heroin addict, but I wasn't bothered by this in the slightest. In fact, it increased my interest in him. I was so naive, I thought that trying heroin might shed some light on my life! We got together, and I thought this 'true love' would make me happy at last. One night he started telling me how a couple of years previously someone had told him about Jesus. I groaned inwardly at the mention of that name, but he went on to explain that something had happened to him deep inside, and he had discovered Jesus was real and alive. I was amazed! This Christianity thing from my childhood, which I had put on hold so many years ago for being 'sad', had affected Mike really deeply. I had to investigate further!

I managed to track down my Bible. I started to read John's Gospel, and the strangest thing happened. It was as though the print on the page was alive. I flicked my eyes over the words and knew this was truth. I started to read about Jesus, and I was gripped. He was amazing. He wasn't the 'irrelevant-to-today' figure that I had in my memory: he was speaking powerful, healing words into people's lives

– people who had the same problems I did! I thought about this for a few days and decided I had to recommit my life to him. I then said sorry for all the wrong things I'd done over the years (this took quite a while). I felt flowing over me the most amazing feeling I have ever had. I can only describe it as 'waves of love' – one wave followed another until I was feeling *so* wonderful. I remember thinking, *This is a hundred times better than taking an 'E'!*

I started going to church, and cut out nearly all drug use. Mike then went into a rehab, which really upset me, and I left my job to move near him. I can see now that this was a mistake, but at the time I was so madly in love with him it felt like the right thing to do. In fact, I would say I was so obsessed with him and with the way of life he represented that, even though I'd had that amazing experience with God, I thought this relationship could offer me more. I tried to get involved in a church, but it seemed there was no one there I could relate to. It was easier to stop going. I felt guilty, as by now I believed totally that Jesus was the way, the truth and the life, and I knew that one day I would be a committed Christian. Mike and I had the right intentions, but when the initial 'high' of becoming Christians wore off and we were faced with things inside ourselves that needed dealing with, instead of looking to God to help us persevere we both looked back to our old obsessions. We moved in together, and soon we were taking drugs and drinking. We moved onto harder drugs, like valium and heavy painkillers. I couldn't help myself, and knew that I was being drawn towards heroin. In a way, I wanted to be. I was getting a kick out of being self-destructive.

Just after I tried methadone for the first time, I found out I was pregnant. What a frightening thing that was – I couldn't even look after myself, let alone a baby! It was a slap in the face, and made me realise what I was doing. I was so thankful to God that I found out I was pregnant before I experimented further with opiates. By the time our child was born, Mike was using large amounts of them. I started using methadone again, and soon became physically addicted. Our lifestyle got more and more out of control. There were nights when we were so heavily drugged, we didn't respond to the baby crying. I was frightened by my addiction, and decided to come off everything. It was an extremely painful withdrawal, and when it was all over I never wanted to touch hard drugs again.

Mike couldn't or wouldn't stop, and eventually I had to leave him because he was becoming violent towards me. What a nightmare! I was homeless and penniless with a baby to look after. I moved around friends' houses for a few weeks and really started to cry out to God. I'd reached the end of myself and had nowhere else to run except to Jesus. In his mercy, he answered my prayers and provided me with somewhere to live near my family. I was deeply depressed, but this time I was determined to follow him – everything I had tried without him had been a disaster. Slowly, with the help of a Christian counsellor and the Holy Spirit, God showed me what made me tick and why, and started to heal my life of the addictions.

That was two and a half years ago. Today I'm a new creation and a very happy, excited person! Jesus is making me whole, and I love him dearly for it. I'm so excited by what he's doing in my life and the lives of people around me. It's amazing that all the excitement and meaning I craved was to be found in Jesus and in his Spirit working inside me.

Like Rebecca, you've probably been told horror stories about what could happen if you ever so much as looked at a drug. Then, when you see people apparently having great fun doing things you'd been told would put you in hospital, prison or a coffin, you wonder what you're missing! Who should you believe? The adults who tell you it'll kill you? Or the drug users who assure you that they're having the time of their life?! I'm sure Rebecca isn't the only Christian teenager who wondered if she was missing out. I did! In the end, she found that following Jesus would have been the best thing to have done all along.

Thirty years ago a man who worked with young people said he thought that drugs posed the biggest threat to teenagers. This warning is still being sounded today. In fact his generation didn't lose it to drugs, so does this mean that we don't need to take them seriously?

I think we do need to take warnings about drugs seriously because drug use is much more widespread now. Crime has doubled in the last ten years as a result. Drugs hurt the people who use them, their families and society in general. We're all affected by the lost potential, the cost to people's health and the rise in crime. Drugs are shaping the lives of entire communities.

What we must realise, however, is that although the teenagers of thirty years ago didn't lose it to drugs, THEY STILL WASTED THEIR POTENTIAL. They sold out, not to drugs, but to materialism and self-advancement. They dedicated their lives to things that have caused damage and waste. This damage isn't as blatant as the harm drugs can do, but materialism hasn't brought the fulfilment it promised. Instead, it has left a trail of broken marriages and dissatisfied people who feel compelled to buy more and more.

Anything that's based on the mentality 'Look after Number One' or 'I'm entitled to feel good' will short-change you, waste your potential and rob you of real joy and purpose. Materialism did that for our parents, and drugs are the most obvious thing around that could do it for us. Even if we never get into drugs, we need to make sure we don't end up overlooking something that can harm us more subtly, as happened with our parents' generation.

This book will help you decide what you think and how you can avoid getting short-changed. Your life is far too important for any of it to be spent in a drunken blur or a drug-induced haze, or even a life-long shopping trip!

2 CRACK THE LIES
The facts on drugs and alcohol

Let's look now at the physical and psychological effects of various drugs, including alcohol, tobacco and solvents.

What is a drug?

The term 'drug' can be used for various natural or man-made substances which affect:

- The body and how it works
- The mind and central nervous system
- Your behaviour and emotions

In this broad sense, alcohol, tobacco and solvents are all drugs.

Some drugs are used for medical reasons – to fight or prevent infection, and to relieve pain or make patients unconscious before they are operated on (anaesthetics). As long as they are used in the right way for the right purpose, the good that these drugs do far outweighs any possible harm.

Drug abuse

Using drugs for non-medical reasons, or in doses larger than recommended, is 'drug abuse' or 'drug misuse'. Using a substance differently from how it's meant to be used, to alter the way you feel, is 'substance misuse' or 'substance abuse'.

Where do drugs come from?

Some drugs are made from plants, eg heroin comes from opium poppies. Others are man-made.

Man-made drugs often have a similar chemical make-up to natural drugs and produce the same effects, but they are cheaper. Some are produced for medical use, others because there's money to be made out of them! The manufacturers of drugs that have no medical use – such as LSD and Ecstasy – might say, 'If people want to buy them, why shouldn't we make them? That's how business works.'

Some drugs used illegally were originally produced for medical use but have been stolen, passed on or sold by the people they were prescribed for. However, most are illegally produced and imported as a way to make money.

Why do people take drugs?

Drugs are usually taken for one or more of the following reasons:

As medicine, to help you recover from illness or to relieve suffering

For pleasure, because it makes you feel good

For religious reasons, because you think it will heighten your spiritual awareness

To be sociable, because it's something people can do together

To improve personal performance

Out of habit, because you have become addicted

For relaxation, to forget your troubles

For cultural reasons, because taking drugs is part of the social custom

When people ask why anyone would take illegal drugs, I guess they mean why do people start when there are so many warnings surrounding drug use. Well, everyone knows that smoking is bad for you, but the risks seem such a long way off. Doesn't lung cancer only happen to the middle-aged?! Most people hate the taste of their first few cigarettes, but they continue because it seems there are some positives to be gained. It's just the same with drugs.

If you wrote a list of the reasons you first did ANYTHING associated with growing up, it might include:

Curiosity
People told you it felt good
Everyone your age was doing it
To look grown up
Didn't want to be 'different'
To rebel or to look like a risk-taker

These are all reasons why people take drugs. We could add:

Boredom
For excitement
To relax
To escape from problems
Felt depressed
Too scared or embarrassed to refuse

Ever done something for one of those reasons? (If you say 'No', I don't believe you.)

What does the law say?

ABOUT DRUGS
The two main laws about drugs are The Medicines Act and The Misuse of Drugs Act.

The Medicines Act says drugs can only be produced and supplied by authorised people. It's therefore illegal to allow your property to be used for the production or supply of drugs. Parents could be prosecuted if drugs exchange hands in their home. The Act makes many drugs 'prescription only', ie they have to be prescribed by a doctor. If they're supplied without a prescription, the next law comes into play.

The Misuse of Drugs Act bans the non-medical use of certain drugs. It places them in different categories, and the penalties for supplying or possessing them depend on what category they're in. This chapter outlines the legal status in 1997 — changes do occur from time to time. At the moment, the maximum penalties are:

Category C
Possession — 2 years' imprisonment, unlimited fine
Supplying — 5 years' imprisonment, unlimited fine.

Category B
Possession — 5 years' imprisonment, unlimited fine.
Supplying — 14 years' imprisonment, unlimited fine.

Category A
Possession — 7 years' imprisonment, unlimited fine.
Supplying — life imprisonment, unlimited fine.

ABOUT TOBACCO
It's illegal (against the law) to sell tobacco to people under 16, but it isn't illegal for people under 16 to smoke.

ABOUT ALCOHOL
It's illegal for children under 5 to be given alcohol, except for medical reasons.

People under 14 aren't allowed into a licensed bar. They may be allowed into other parts of a pub.

It's illegal to sell alcohol to anyone under 18. People under 18 aren't allowed to drink alcohol on licensed premises, unless they are having a meal and only then if they are over 16 years old. Anyone under 18 can be fined up to £200 if they are caught buying alcohol or drinking in a bar.

It's illegal to be drunk and disorderly in a public place — 5,000 under-18s are convicted (found guilty in court) of this each year. Some towns have local bye-laws that ban people from drinking in public places.

It's legal to make alcoholic drinks at home, but illegal to sell them.

ABOUT SOLVENTS

It's illegal to sell solvents to anyone under 18 if there is reason to believe they will inhale them. It's illegal to sell solvents to anyone over 18 if there is reason to believe they will give them to someone under 18 to abuse.

Solvent sniffers can be arrested for unruly or offensive behaviour.

Some definitions
• • • • • • • • • • • • • • • • • • •

Later in the book we'll need to use some jargon:

tolerance
The body gets used to (tolerates) alcohol and most drugs after a while, so more has to be taken to get the same effect. Developing tolerance to a drug will put you at greater risk of its toxic (poisonous) effects.

withdrawals
If certain drugs are used regularly, the body will adapt by

altering the way the brain and nervous system work. If drug use stops suddenly, the body can't cope when the residue leaves the system, and 'withdrawal symptoms' result. These vary depending on the drug, but can include being sick, hallucinating, feeling paranoid and very weak. They continue while the body adapts to not having the drug any more.

Not all drugs cause physical withdrawal; but because our bodies, emotions and minds are interrelated, people who stop any sort of regular drug use may experience some sort of withdrawal – they may not be able to sleep, or feel anxious or depressed.

addiction

Although this book focuses on addiction to chemicals (drugs, alcohol, tobacco and solvents) you will find that it is relevant to any addiction. People can be addicted to all sorts of things: shopping, gambling, porn, work, even chocolate!

Addiction can begin as an insignificant event, eg eating a bar of chocolate to console yourself after being teased at school. If this behaviour is repeated several times within a short space of time, it can become a habit. The estimate is that it takes three weeks to make a habit and six weeks to break it.

Addiction can be viewed as a habit over which the person has lost control – the habit rules them, rather than the other way around. I am certainly not saying drug addiction is the same as ANY bad habit you can't break, but many of us have the potential to become addicted to SOMETHING.

It can be very hard to understand why addicted people do the things they do. Sometimes it seems as though they've gone through a complete personality change. Some people have described addiction as a love affair.

He has fallen in love. This drug seems to offer what he's always been looking for. As his love grows, the drug comes to mean more to him than anything else. So he gives up the other things that were important to him so that he can devote more time to the one he loves.

It's a passionate affair. Sometimes the drug causes him pain, but he's so in love he's quick to forgive and forget. Everything else seems less important. Friends and relatives express concern, and try to tell him where it's all leading. But he doesn't believe that the one he loves could be out to destroy him.

Occasionally, when his love has really hurt him, he starts to doubt that this is true love. Then the good feelings come back and he finds he cannot end the relationship. He hangs on in the hope that things will once again be like the blissful days when they first met. Even if his love does hurt him, being together still seems so much better than being apart…

(Sounds like the script for a corny film, doesn't it?)

PHYSICAL ADDICTION – When the body gets used to having a particular drug in it, the user will suffer withdrawals when he or she stops taking it.

EMOTIONAL/PSYCHOLOGICAL ADDICTION – This happens when a person needs the drug just to feel 'normal', or to avoid depression or anxiety. People keep taking drugs like cocaine to try to recapture the good feeling they got when they first took it.

What do drugs do?

Drugs are often divided into four categories according to how they affect your body:

1 **Stimulants** cause your brain (and therefore the rest of your body) to speed up.
2 **Deliriants** (solvents and gases) have a stimulant effect followed by a sedative one.
3 **Hallucinogens** change the way the brain works so that you perceive things differently.
4 **Depressants** sedate your brain so that your central nervous system slows down.

There isn't space here to tell you everything there is to know about every drug. I will give you the main facts about those most commonly abused in the UK.

1 STIMULANTS

Cocaine

Slang names
Coke, Snow, Charlie.

What is it?
A white powder made from the coca plant.

Effects
An instant feeling of euphoria that lasts 5–30 minutes. Feelings of confidence and power. The user can think more quickly and doesn't feel pain. But the high may give way to panic and anxiety, and the user may become violent.

Short-term risks
Cocaine is very addictive. Once the high wears off, depression sets in and the user may want to take more. Death can

occur from heart and respiratory failure. Overdoses may lead to seizures and death. Large doses, or using it for several hours at a time, can cause hallucinations and psychosis (mental illness).

Long-term risks
Euphoria is replaced by restlessness, hyper-excitability and sickness. This may develop into a state of mind similar to mental illness. The nose and teeth rot. Regular use reduces general health, resulting in sleeplessness and weight loss.

Is it addictive?
There are psychological and physical withdrawals. People become dependent on the heroic feelings cocaine creates. They may use it to avoid the fatigue and depression they feel when they stop.

Crack

Slang names
Pebbles, Scud, Rock, Wash, Stone.

What is it?
Cocaine that has been chemically altered to form smokeable crystals.

Effects
The same as cocaine. Crack makes you feel relaxed and mentally alert. But users may experience loss of control over their thoughts and be unable to talk properly.

Risks
Crack is a very short-acting drug resulting in compulsive use as the person tries to recapture the initial high. It can damage the lungs.

What does the law say?
Cocaine is 'prescription only' and a Class A controlled drug.
Coca leaf and Crack are not available for medical use.

Amphetamine sulphate

Slang names
Speed, Whizz, Uppers, Billy, Sulphate.

What is it?
A man-made white, grey or pinkish powder, pill or capsule.
Amphetamines were prescribed in the 1950s and 1960s for
depression and to promote weight loss. They are now
rarely prescribed because of the bad side-effects and the
fact that people were easily addicted.

Effects
Amphetamine acts on the central nervous system in a similar way to adrenaline. Breathing and the heart rate speed
up. The high lasts for about 2 hours, producing feelings of
confidence and energy. The user becomes rather talkative.
The drug lessens the desire to eat and sleep. Feelings of
anxiety often follow. High doses can lead to panic attacks,
and the body may take days to recover.

Short-term risks
The longer you're up, the longer you'll be down. Users feel
tired and depressed after the high is over. It's never enough
– to keep getting the same effect you have to take more
and more. Sniffing amphetamine damages the nose. The
drug may be heavily cut (mixed with other substances) –
often only about 5%, and very rarely more than 25%, of
what you get is amphetamine: the rest could be chalk,
scouring powder or who knows what.

Long-term risks
The amount you need can increase 10–20 times – it becomes very expensive! There is a risk of tremors, ulcers, loss of coordination, blurred vision, anxiety and skin disorders. Users may experience confusion and lack of confidence. Resistance to illness is reduced. There is risk of heart failure and damage to the heart due to raised blood pressure. Using large amounts in one go produces toxic effects, eg hallucinations, paranoia and permanent brain damage.

Is it addictive?
Withdrawals are mental rather than physical, and addiction is psychological rather than physical. The user may experience cravings and depression.

What does the law say?
A 'prescription only' medication and a Class B controlled drug. If prepared for injection, it becomes Class A.

Tobacco

What is it?
Tobacco plants are dried for smoking. They contain nicotine which is a stimulant and addictive. 85% of people who try tobacco become addicted, often after only 5–10 cigarettes.

Effects
The heart rate increases by up to 40%. Blood pressure increases. Chemicals that cause cancer are released into the bloodstream, the brain and the central nervous system.

Risks
Cancer, breathing problems, damage to unborn children – you've heard them hundreds of times, I'm sure! It's estimated that 100,000 deaths each year in this country are caused by smoking tobacco. Once addicted, people feel

agitated when they start to withdraw. Smoking then has a relaxing effect as it eases the withdrawals.

2 DELIRIANTS (SOLVENTS & GASES)

'Once, after I'd been sniffing *Tippex*, I started hallucinating and thought I saw a load of policemen charging through the bushes after me. I was so terrified, I ran four miles to get away, not even looking before I crossed roads.' *(Emma)*

What are they?
'Solvents' fall into three categories:

◎ Volatile solvents found in glue, petrol, lighter fuel and cleaning fluids
◎ Aerosols (deodorant, hairspray, insecticide)
◎ Anaesthetics (ether and chloroform)

Effects
Solvents take effect very quickly and wear off after 15–45 minutes. The stimulating effect is similar to being drunk, and is followed by drowsiness. Big doses can lead to total loss of control and hallucinations.

Short-term risks
Solvents cause more deaths than any other illegal drug, 50% of them due to the toxic effect of the substance used. Gas or aerosols freeze air passages, causing suffocation, and users can die from choking, heart failure or accident. Other effects are sickness, nosebleeds, stomach cramps, a rash around the nose and mouth, sore eyes and hallucinations.

Long-term risks
There is permanent damage to the central nervous system, causing panic attacks and paranoia. There may also be damage to the brain, bone marrow, kidneys and liver.

Are they addictive?
Solvent users may become mentally dependent and experience withdrawals.

GHB

Slang
GBH, Liquid E.

What is it?
Gamma hydroxyl butyrate, a man-made mixture of solvents and caustic soda. The drug is inhaled.

Effects
These vary depending on the 'recipe'. The drug may do nothing, or it may cause extreme loss of sexual inhibition, shakes in the arm and leg muscles, collapse, coma or death. You don't know which you'll get till you try! Many users end up needing emergency medical treatment.

3 HALLUCINOGENS

LSD

'Sometimes it means hours of terror. You think you're going to die, and there's nothing you can do to come back out of it.' *(Emma)*

Slang names
Acid, Trips, Tabs.

What is it?
LSD is derived from ergot, a fungus that grows on rye. It is a white powder, usually mixed to form a liquid. In the UK, LSD comes on small 'stamps' of blotting paper or card (blotters), thin gelatine squares or bright tablets

(microdots). The drug was used in the 1950s and 1960s by psychologists to try to help patients recover buried memories, but was made illegal because of the damage it caused.

Effects
This depends on the size of the dose, the environment and the user's mood. The 'trip' starts after approximately 1 hour, peaks after 5–6 and diminishes after 8. LSD alters the way the mind processes incoming data, so that sights, sensations and sounds that usually seem trivial become very important. There is distortion of vision and hearing, a feeling of being outside the body, and changes in the perception of time and place. Some people find it mystical, others find it terrifying. Tolerance develops rapidly with frequent use. The user may feel very fatigued when the trip is over.

Risks
Acid can trigger underlying mental illness. There may be lasting anxiety states, panic attacks and personality changes. LSD may not be spread evenly, so half a 'stamp' doesn't mean half the dose. Bad trips bring depression, dizziness, panic and confusion. Behaviour can become dangerous. Flashbacks – short-lived, vivid 'memories' of previous trips – may occur. There may be psychological damage after repeated use.

What does the law say?
Not available for medical use. A Class A controlled drug.

Magic Mushrooms

What are they?
Liberty Cap and Fly Agaric mushrooms contain psilocybin which has hallucinogenic properties. These mushrooms grow in the wild in the UK. They can be eaten raw, dried or cooked.

Effects

Low doses cause feelings of happiness and detachment. The user becomes relaxed and talkative. High doses will probably lead to distorted vision and hallucinations. The strength of these depends on the number of mushrooms eaten.

Short-term risks

Bad trips bring panic, anxiety and loss of control which can lead to destructive behaviour. The user may suffer acute stomach ache. People have died from poisoning after eating the wrong type of mushrooms.

Long-term risks

Memory impairment and trouble with abstract thinking. There is the possibility of brain damage.

Are they addictive?

No, but people can come to rely on mushrooms as a way to feel sociable.

What does the law say?

There are no controls on raw mushrooms, but if they are prepared for eating they become a Class A drug.

Ecstasy

'You're everything you ever wanted to be, then suddenly the plug's pulled out.' *(Rosie)*

Slang names

'E', numerous 'brand names', eg Disco Burgers, Fantasy, Love Doves, New Yorkers, Adam, M25s.

What is it?

A man-made substance, chemically known as MDMA, with several chemical variations. It has amphetamine-like and hallucinogenic properties. About half the 'Ecstasy' seized by police contains no Ecstasy at all, but is amphetamine, keta-mine or nothing. The drug comes as a tablet or capsule, occasionally as a powder.

Effects
Ecstasy produces feelings of warmth, confidence, friendliness and extra energy. Sensations are enhanced, and people feel less inhibited and as if they understand others better. But sometimes hallucinations and nausea occur.

Short-term risks
Large amounts make you anxious, confused and paranoid. The body temperature rises, and energetic dancing in a hot place without drinking enough can lead to heat stroke and dehydration. Avoid this by taking breaks and having frequent small drinks. (But don't drink a lot of liquid in one go – that has killed people too!) Don't drink alcohol, as this may result in dehydration. People have died from this and from what is believed to be an allergic reaction to the drug.

'E' affects coordination, so it's dangerous to drive. It alters chemicals in the brain, so when it wears off the user may feel depressed. The drug is very dangerous if you have a heart condition, epilepsy, high blood pressure, asthma or are on anti-depressants. 'E' has all the risks of other stimulants and hallucinogens, plus unpredictability.

Long-term risks
Not much is recorded medically about the effects of long-term use. Only time will tell! Symptoms like those of Parkinson's Disease can develop – tremors, impaired speech, paralysis. Other risks include liver damage, sleeplessness and general poor health. Women may suffer from heavy periods.

What does the law say?
Not available for medical use. A Class A controlled drug.

Cannabis

'I know someone whose husband thought he could fly after drinking cannabis tea. He ended up killing their baby and later committed suicide in prison.'
(Debbie)

What is it?
Cannabis is derived from the hemp plant and used in three forms:

◎ Herbal cannabis (grass, weed, pot, marijuana, dope, ganga) is made from the dried plant. Sinsemilla, made from the flowering top of the unfertilised plant, is stronger.

◎ Cannabis resin (hash, draw, blow, puff) is scraped from the dried plant and compressed into dark-coloured blocks.

◎ Cannabis oil.

THC is the chemical substance in cannabis that causes the effects. Skunk is a species of cannabis with a high level of THC.

Effects
Like alcohol, cannabis stimulates the nervous system before depressing it. In small quantities, the senses are enhanced; people feel relaxed or stimulated, more friendly or giggly. However, large quantities lead to sickness, hallucinations, panic and paranoia. You are likely to feel worse if you take cannabis when depressed or anxious. If you eat or drink the drug, and are badly affected, it's too late to do anything about it. Cannabis can set off underlying mental illness in some people. The reflexes slow down, leading to an increased risk of having or causing an accident.

Short-term risks
THC remains in the brain for up to a week, longer than any other drug. It affects how the brain transfers information from one nerve cell to another, making short-term memory less effective and slowing down the ability to learn. There may be a lack of concentration and difficulty in thinking straight.

Long-term risks
ON THE BRAIN – THC stays in the grey matter, hindering abstract thought. Some long-term users can't distinguish between abstract and concrete thinking. The drug reduces performance at work or school and the ability to cope with new situations or with frustration. Emotional responses become distorted. Users tend to become apathetic towards life.

ON THE LUNGS – Cannabis smoke contains about 50% more cancer-causing hydrocarbons than tobacco. It goes deeper into the lungs and is absorbed differently from nicotine, so it can impair the function of the lungs. Like tobacco, cannabis causes bronchitis and throat problems.

ON REPRODUCTION – Men and women become less fertile. Women are more likely to miscarry if they're using cannabis regularly.

Because cannabis hasn't been used as widely as tobacco, there is not yet much conclusive evidence of how it affects other parts of the body. Some people think it may affect the liver and the heart, and cause genetic malformation in children born to those who have smoked it heavily. More research is needed. A huge majority of hard-drug users began with cannabis.

Is it addictive?
It is psychologically addictive, and the body does develop a

tolerance. Studies in countries where cannabis is used culturally have shown that after approximately twenty years people need six times more to get the same effect. When they stop using cannabis, some people experience insomnia, nausea and irritability for a couple of days afterwards.

What the law says?
Medical use is not permitted. This is a Class B controlled drug. Cannabis oil is Class A.

Paul

Everyone knows about the good feelings dope gives, but the negative effects are rarely mentioned. It has taken years for me to realise fully the negative effects of dope on my life and to break free.

It began with the feeling that nothing really mattered. This led to me always being late, not caring about my appearance or the clothes I was wearing. Work seemed like a pain, and I did just enough to get by. I became completely apathetic towards everything and everyone.

I smoked dope in order to feel better, yet it made me even more unhappy. I made promises to myself every day about giving up and working harder, but they never came to anything. I had no vision for the future. Dope made me totally confused about everything in my life, ranging from the people I liked to the food I ate. I became insecure, nervous about meeting new people or doing new things.

The more I felt like this, the more I smoked. It

wasn't until I started to look closely at my friends that it dawned on me they had been smoking for years and had nothing. Most of all, underneath the laughing that happens after a good smoke, every one of them was deeply unhappy and could see no way out. Because of the demotivating effect dope has, they saw little chance of escaping that way of life other than through the high another joint gives.

Dope is anti-life. The high it gives is just a false promise of the good times it actually takes away. It has taken sixteen years for me to break free from my addiction to it – half my life!

4 DEPRESSANTS (NARCOTICS)

Narcotics depress the central nervous system and are used to reduce pain.

OPIATES are made from opium poppies. Heroin is the best known of these. It comes as a brown/white powder which may be cut (mixed) with chalk, flour or who knows what. Opiates are prescribed as painkillers, and have a medical use as a cough suppressant and anti-diarrhoea agent. Like all sedatives, opiates depress the central nervous system. Doctors have to inform the Home Office of people who are addicted. There are 28,000 registered addicts in Britain, but it is believed the true figure is five times higher.

OPIOIDS are man-made versions of opiates, including methadone, pethidine and diconal. Methadone is often pre-scribed to help heroin addicts come off the drug, but unfor-tunately it's also addictive and has longer-lasting withdrawals than heroin. Opioids are used medically as painkillers.

ANALGESICS – the best known of these is codeine which is in some cough mixtures. Analgesics have a similar chemical make-up to opiates and opioids, but aren't nearly as powerful.

Heroin

Slang names
H, Smack, Brown.

Effects
The initial euphoric high is followed by feelings of relaxation and contentment, especially when injected. (If other narcotics are used above the recommended dose, they have similar effects and risks.)

Risks
Addiction to heroin is guaranteed after repeated use. Once someone is addicted, the pleasure of using the drug is replaced by the relief it gives from withdrawals. Overdose can lead to convulsions or death.

Is it addictive?
The body develops a tolerance for the drug and the user becomes physically addicted. Withdrawals include a runny nose, the sweats, cramps and a psychological craving for more.

What does the law say?
Narcotics are 'prescription only' medication. Heroin, morphine, methadone, diconal and pethidine are Class A drugs. Codeine and DF118 are Class B, but if they are prepared for injection they become Class A. Distalgesic and temgesic are Class C. Some very dilute mixtures, eg cough mixture, can be bought without a prescription.

amyl and butyl nitrate

'I felt like a belt was being pulled tight round my head, and that my heart would burst out of my chest.' *(Rosie)*

Slang names
Poppers, various 'brand names', eg Rave, Hi-Tech.

What is it?
A man-made fluid similar to laughing gas, mainly prescribed for angina because it increases the heart rate.

Effects
Nitrates cause an instant short 'rush' – the blood vessels relax, the heart rate increases, the face flushes. Users may experience light-headedness (and are therefore more likely to have or cause accidents) and headaches.

Risks
Large doses cause sickness, delirium, decreased heart and breathing rate, low blood pressure and fainting. People have died from drinking nitrates. Not much is known about long-term effects. Some think there may be an increased risk of cancer.

What does the law say?
Amyl nitrate is a pharmacy medication. There are no legal controls over the use of butyl nitrate.

Ketamine

'I know someone who is scarred for life, because he didn't realise he was burning himself all up the back of his legs and torso. Another bloke went blind for a few days.' *(Debbie)*

Slang names
Special K, Vitamin K, White Diamond, Kit Kat, Green.

What is it?
An anaesthetic with analgesic (painkilling) and psychedelic (mind altering) properties. Ketamine is used by vets to anaesthetise animals. It comes in the form of white tablets, a powder, and red & white or gold & white capsules. If it has been stolen from a vet, it may come ready for injection!

Effects
There is an initial 'rush' of energy followed by a feeling of detachment from your surroundings, slurred speech, blurred vision, vomiting, numbness or paralysis. The effects can be similar to LSD, along with a floating or flying feeling. But ketamine differs from LSD in that it often causes aggressive behaviour.

Risks
The user may have strong hallucinations and, later, flash-backs. Because ketamine is an anaesthetic, people can damage themselves without realising what they're doing. Many have bad trips, enduring terrifying hallucinations that seem very real. Large doses can lead to heart failure. Frequent or prolonged use can produce mental illness.

Is it addictive?
The body develops a tolerance, and the user risks becoming psychologically dependent on the drug.

What does the law say?
Ketamine is a 'prescription only' medicine.

Sedative hypnotics

Slang names
Jellies, Eggs, Tranx, Sleeping pills.

What are they?

Sedatives calm people down. Hypnotics induce sleep. They are prescribed by doctors for depression or insomnia. The effects outlined here occur when the drugs are abused, ie used in larger amounts than recommended or by people who don't need them.

There are two categories: barbiturates and benzodiazipines (eg valium, temazepam, diazepam). Barbiturates have more or less been replaced by benzodiazipines. They come as tablets and capsules.

Effects

Sedative hypnotics depress the central nervous system. The effects last for 3–6 hours. Small doses make people feel relaxed and sociable. Reflexes are slowed, and judgement is impaired – there is an increased risk of accident. With larger doses, the sedative effects take over, resulting in depression, anxiety, extreme and unpredictable emotional reactions, and confusion. There is a great risk of overdose, leading to death, particularly when the drugs are mixed with alcohol.

Is it addictive?

It's easy to develop psychological dependence. Withdrawals are worse than heroin – panic and convulsions that may be fatal.

What does the law say?

Sedative hypnotics are a 'prescription only' medicine. Barbiturates are Class B. Benzodiazipines are Class C. It is not illegal to possess them without a prescription, but if they are given or sold without a prescription they become Class C.

anabolic steroids

What are they?
They are derived from the male hormone, testosterone, and are sometimes prescribed to help people build up muscle after an illness.

Effects
They increase muscle bulk and improve performance where muscle strength is needed (eg athletics, weightlifting). But they also stimulate aggression.

Risks
Mood changes, aggression, heart disease, high blood pressure, depression, acne, hair loss. The drug has been known to affect the reproductive organs and sex hormones. Men may become impotent and develop breasts. Women can develop masculine characteristics which remain even if they stop taking the drug. Steroids prevent young people growing properly, damage the liver and may cause liver cancer.

What does the law say?
A 'prescription only' medicine and a Class A controlled drug.

alcohol

What is it?
Alcoholic drinks are made by fermenting or distilling natural substances until alcohol forms.

- Wine is usually made from grapes and has a 6–14% alcohol content.
- Beer is made from grains with a 4–6% alcohol content.
- Spirits are made by distilling fermented grain or potatoes, and have a 40–50% alcohol content.

Effects

This depends on the percentage of alcohol in the drink. The drinks in the illustration below contain the same amount of alcohol (1 unit).

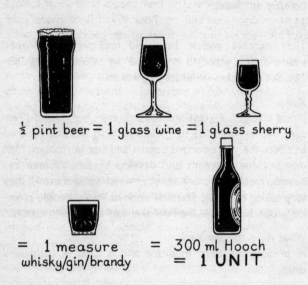

½ pint beer = 1 glass wine = 1 glass sherry

= 1 measure whisky/gin/brandy = 300 ml Hooch = 1 UNIT

Alcohol is usually measured in units. The number of units a drink amounts to is calculated by multiplying the volume by the alcohol content and dividing it by 1,000. For example, a 330 ml bottle of Hooch is 330 x 4.7% (its alcohol content) ÷ 1,000 = 1.55 units.

Alcohol is a depressant that sedates the brain and central nervous system. This sedative effect makes people lose their inhibitions, which is why at first they feel more 'alive' and confident.

When the alcohol first enters the stomach, some of it is absorbed straight into the bloodstream. This is why you get drunk quickly if you drink on an empty stomach. If there is food in the stomach, particularly carbohydrate, the alcohol is absorbed more slowly and has more chance of being broken down by the liver first. The liver breaks it down at a fixed speed of about one unit per hour. If you drink more, your liver can't get rid of it any faster, so you get drunk quicker.

If you drink more than your body can cope with at one time, alcohol will poison you. This is why people are often sick when they've had too much – the stomach wants to get rid of it the quickest way possible! 1,000 people under 15 are admitted to hospital each year suffering from alcohol poisoning. Many of them die.

Once alcohol is in the bloodstream and the level of sedation is increasing in the brain, feelings of depression and emotional instability come to the surface. Gradually, the overall sedative effect takes hold and people become sleepy or, at high levels, unconscious. Alcohol slows down breathing. Large amounts may lead to respiratory failure.

The amount of alcohol your body can cope with varies according to your age, your body weight, how quickly you drank it, and whether you are used to drinking. The rate of absorption is quicker in women (ie they get drunk faster), and in the long term women develop organ damage more readily than men. This is partly because alcohol isn't absorbed by fat cells. If women are on the contraceptive pill, they are more likely to get drunk. Bearing in mind that everyone is different, the illustration on page 43 shows how different amounts of alcohol may affect behaviour.

If you drink excessively, alcohol can remain in the body for hours afterwards. You may have had a few hours' sleep and still be unsafe to drive. The ways people try to 'sober up' (eg by drinking black coffee) don't get rid of the alcohol any quicker. Nothing will make the liver work faster.

Hangovers are caused partly by poisoning and partly by dehydration and low blood sugar. The additive that causes the poisoning is present in larger quantities in darker drinks such as brandy and red wine.

Alcoholic soft drinks ('Alcopops')

In the last year, alcopops have raked in about £250 million for their manufacturers. Many more will appear over the next year or so, becoming increasingly imaginative in what they look like and what they contain! But what are they?

The exact contents vary, but alcopops are usually made from distilled or fermented fruit, or fruit juice with alcohol or liqueur added. Although many of them don't taste like alcohol, they have at least 4–5.5% alcohol content. They are as strong as or stronger than beer. It should say on the bottle what the alcohol content is, and it is wise to check this. Just because it's a tiny bottle doesn't mean it won't have much effect!

Risks
Alcohol is high in calories and bad for your complexion! Drinking alcohol in small amounts poses no risk to health, but increases your chances of having or causing an accident. This doubles if you drive after having a drink, even though

2 UNITS
LOSS OF JUDGEMENT, INCREASED RISK OF ACCIDENT, REDUCED INHIBITIONS, RELAXED FEELING.

3-4 UNITS
INCREASED LOSS OF INHIBITIONS, REDUCED CO-ORDINATION, CHEERFULNESS, SLOW REACTIONS.

8-10 UNITS
LOSS OF SELF-CONTROL, QUARRELSOME, DIFFICULTY WALKING.

10-12 UNITS
EXPERIENCING DOUBLE VISION, STAGGERING, MEMORY LOSS, PARALYSIS LEADING TO COMA, DEATH.

you may be below the legal limit. An inexperienced driver is five times more likely to have an accident, even when under the alcohol limit.

It takes a while to discover how much alcohol your body can cope with, which means young people are more susceptible to accidents or poisoning.

Mixing drinks often makes you sick because the body is unable to cope with the combined ingredients. It won't make you get drunker – it's the alcohol content that determines that. Mixing alcohol with fizzy drinks causes you to get drunk more quickly because the fizz penetrates the stomach lining faster. So if you haven't eaten for a while and have a fizzy drink containing alcohol, the effects may be more drastic than you expect!

Mixing alcohol with drugs is extremely dangerous (particularly if the drug is a sedative). The combination has a much stronger effect and causes many accidental deaths.

People tend to do things they later regret when they are drunk. Many end up in sexual encounters that are embarrassing or worse, with strangers or people they would never have had sex with if they were sober. I have met several people (men and women) who were raped when they were drunk, who are convinced it wouldn't have happened if they hadn't been drinking. There is a saying that our conscience is alcohol-soluble, and most people end up doing things when drunk that they wouldn't normally do.

Alcohol causes around 30,000 deaths each year in Britain. Some people die because they have become ill by drinking too much over a long period of time. Many more die in accidents – alcohol-related car accidents are the highest cause of death among young people. 65% of suicide attempts are made by people who have been drinking, and suicide attempts involving alcohol are more likely to succeed. Alcohol is a key factor in half of all deaths in fires, one-third of drownings, two-thirds of manslaughter charges, and nearly half of all burglaries and robberies.

Is it addictive?
Between 5–10% of 'social drinkers' become alcoholics, ie addicted to alcohol. This causes physical problems such as

stomach ulcers and liver failure, together with the other kinds of suffering that addiction triggers. Researchers believe there may be a genetic factor which makes the bodies of some people deal with alcohol differently, and which puts them at a higher risk of becoming alcoholic.

It takes most people a long time to become addicted to alcohol, but young people who drink large amounts seem to become addicted more rapidly. New drinkers usually have a low tolerance for alcohol – they get drunk quickly or feel ill, so they don't drink much. But some people, particularly those with alcoholic parents, find they can drink much more before they get drunk or feel ill – they have a high tolerance. This may lend them some street cred, so they continue. But their bodies are gradually adapting to alcohol, and before long they will need to drink just to feel okay. Eventually the body's ability to handle alcohol breaks down – the tolerance level decreases – but if the drinker stops completely he will suffer withdrawals because he will have become addicted. So someone who can't drink much is at risk of accident and poisoning, while someone who can drink a lot is at risk of becoming addicted without realising it.

>→⊪⊪ >→⊪⊪ >→⊪⊪
• • • • • • • • • • • • • • •

Safe drinking

The following advice is for those who want to drink alcohol in a way that minimises their chances of it having any adverse consequences.

Doctors recommend that adult men don't drink more than 21 units per week, and women no more than 14, to avoid health damage or becoming addicted. They also recommend having at least one alcohol-free day each week. These are adult limits: young people's bodies can't cope with this much.

Buy half-pints or small measures, as this will encourage you to drink less.

It's sensible to eat something before you drink.

Drink slowly. Putting your glass down between gulps, rather than holding it, will help.

Intersperse alcoholic drinks with non-alcoholic ones.

Local sources of help

✦ Look for an advert in your local paper.
✦ Ask the Samaritans (see local phone directory)
✦ Ask the Citizens Advice Bureau (see phone book)
✦ Write to the Standing Committee on Drugs and Alcohol (SCODA) at1–4 Hatton Place, Hatton Garden, London EC1N 8ND. Enclose a large stamped addressed envelope.

What to do in an emergency

IF SOMEONE IS UNCONSCIOUS:

☺ Put him in the recovery position or on his side.
☺ Make sure he can breathe.
☺ Call an ambulance.
☺ Show the ambulance crew anything he may have taken.

IF SOMEONE IS HAVING A BAD TRIP:

◎ Talk calmly and reassuringly.
◎ If possible, take him to a place where it's quiet with subdued lighting, where he feels comfortable.

46

- ◎ Find a friend or someone he can trust, who can reassure him.
- ◎ Keep talking, reassuring him that what he's experiencing is drug-induced and not real.
- ◎ Remember – you may be there for some time. Depending on how much he has taken, it could be up to twelve hours!
- ◎ If he becomes uncontrollable or hysterical, call a doctor. Remember that this, or being taken to hospital, may make him even more panicky, so only do it as a last resort.

When dancing, people can collapse or become faint after taking drugs such as Ecstasy, Speed or Poppers. If someone does this, he may be suffering from heat stroke or dehydration:

- ☹ Take him to a place where he can cool down.
- ☹ Give him water to drink, NEVER ALCOHOL – it'll dehydrate him even more.
- ☹ Use water to cool down his face and neck.
- ☹ If he's unconscious, call an ambulance straight away – there may be something more seriously wrong.

OTHER FORMS OF INTOXICATION:

- ℮ If he's lying down, put him on his side in case he is sick. Loosen any tight clothing.
- ℮ Don't give him anything to eat or drink, unless you suspect that he is dehydrated, in which case give him water to drink.
- ℮ Make sure he is safe – have someone stay with him if necessary.
- ℮ Bearing in mind that it's not helpful to shield people from the consequences of their chemical use (unless this particular trip is life or health threatening), ask him later to clear up any mess and pay for any damage done.

3 SPEEDING WHERE?
The road to addiction

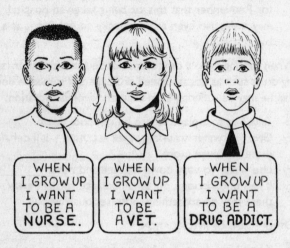

WHEN I GROW UP I WANT TO BE A **NURSE.**

WHEN I GROW UP I WANT TO BE **A VET.**

WHEN I GROW UP I WANT TO BE A **DRUG ADDICT.**

Have you ever heard anyone say that? Out of the hundreds of addicts I've met, only one wanted to get addicted. So what happened to the others?

Many of you will know people who take drugs occasionally and who aren't addicted. A lot of people use drugs for a while and then 'grow out of it'. The trouble is, no one can accurately predict where and when they will stop. At fifteen, Rebecca had no intention of ever doing anything more than pot. Her story showed how becoming addicted was a gradual process; she didn't even notice what was happening.

Drug use is enjoyable at first. People feel they have it under control and it's not causing any problems. However, after a while users discover that the drug they are taking starts to turn on them.

Why go on after you have had a bad experience? It seems crazy. The reason people continue is because the drug seems to offer a 'solution' for something, and this 'solution' is good enough to make it worth putting up with any problems that come with it. As time goes by, the drug will alter a person's way of looking at reality and eventually he or she can't see that there's a problem at all. Drug users rationalise their behaviour ('I only smoke dope to unwind after a hard day'), blame others ('I got drunk because my girlfriend kept eyeing up everyone else'), minimise it ('I'm not as bad as Uncle Fred'), or just deny what happened ('I didn't cause the crash – it was the other guy'). Very slowly, without noticing it, the user starts to need the drug. Taking it, even with all the hassle involved, feels better than the physical or mental pain that results otherwise.

The road to addiction

We have already seen how drugs and alcohol alter the way you feel. The road to addiction (see p50) could be described in terms of how the drug affects the user's mood.[1]

Most people don't get beyond stage two. But remember, those who end up in stages three or four intended to stop earlier. Research suggests that the younger you are when you start, the quicker you tend to progress through the stages.

Let's look at each stage in more detail, with the help of an imaginary 'totally average bloke' called Dave.

1 FINDS MOOD SWING

2 SEEKS MOOD SWING

3 USING TO ESCAPE

4 USING TO FEEL NORMAL

STAGE 1 – FINDING THE MOOD SWING

what does he take?

Dave has his first 'proper drink' at a friend's house, sharing a four-pack with a group of friends. He likes the way it makes him feel, and he wants to socialise in adult ways. So he and his friends continue to drink a few cans together now and again.

what happens?

Dave discovers he can alter how he feels by drinking. Apart from having a hangover once, he experiences no problems, and his parents don't suspect anything.

At this stage Dave is using alcohol because:

☺ It's fun; he likes the feeling and being in a good mood
☺ He's curious
☺ He likes to take risks

Typical features of this stage:

☻ People only use now and again
☻ Tolerance is low, and they don't need much to get an effect
☻ Usually there are no adverse consequences (there is still an increased risk of accidents and people may have frightening/dangerous reactions to drugs such as LSD)

STAGE 2 – SEEKING THE MOOD SWING

what does he take?

After getting drunk at a party, Dave is in so much trouble with his parents that he doesn't drink for six weeks. Then at a friend's house one Saturday, he remembers how he enjoyed the feeling of being drunk and decides he doesn't want to miss out any more. Over the summer holidays he starts hanging around with neighbours who drink more than him and who smoke dope.

When the new term starts, Dave gets into a pattern of drinking and smoking dope most weekends and sometimes mid-week. He makes rules for himself to control his use, eg 'I'll only get drunk at weekends' and 'I'll only smoke dope, never anything else'.

how does he behave?

Dave starts getting into trouble for not doing homework, and a few months later he starts skipping classes. He lies to his parents and gives vague explanations about where he's going and who with. He spends more and more time and energy thinking about when he can next get drunk. He has stopped going to church because he needs a lie-in after Saturday night, and he enjoys spending time with his new friends rather than with the church youth group. When he gets into trouble as a result of his chemical use, he blames something or someone else.

Dave's reasons for using chemicals now are:

☹ Most of his friends use them
☹ Life isn't much fun otherwise
☹ He doesn't see that it causes any problems

Typical features of this stage include:

☺ Increased tolerance – it takes more of the substance to produce an effect
☺ Development of a 'routine' when the user will drink or take drugs
☺ The person creates rules about what he or she will use
☺ A change in friends – users now mix with people who take chemicals in the same way that they do
☺ Social events are seen as an opportunity to drink or take drugs
☺ There are clashes between the person's chemical use and his or her personal or spiritual values

Stage 3 – Using to Escape

what does he take?

A year or so later Dave is in the habit of getting wrecked every weekend and using chemicals several times in the week, particularly to help him through the 'come down' from the weekend. His tolerance for alcohol has grown and he needs much more to get drunk. He likes to try out new buzzes, so he takes whatever drugs come his way.

how does he behave?

Over the last year Dave has made a lot of changes in his life because of his drug and alcohol use. His grades have gone down, he has left the football team (training took up too much time), and he doesn't feel guilty any more about lying to his parents. His values have changed so that he now does things he previously thought were wrong. His friends include older people, some of whom are heavy drug users. He has got increasingly sneaky with his parents. When they do catch him out, he promises he'll stop – but he never does. He steals money to buy drugs, gets into fights and can't sleep properly. But he keeps people at a distance by pretending everything is okay. If anyone suggests that he's got a problem, he denies it. He either makes it seem less serious than it really is, or he blames it on someone else. Using drugs has become his Number One priority and he looks forward to it all week. He sacrifices his relationships with his family and friends to his relationship with chemicals.

what's going on inside him?

Dave is starting to think that maybe he has less control over or choice about when or how much he'll use. Sometimes he only intends to have a couple of cans, but gets drunk anyway. He starts to break his own rules. When he isn't under the influence of chemicals, he becomes depressed. He feels different from other people and cut off from them. Sometimes he feels guilty and ashamed about how he's living, but this is too uncomfortable to think about for long.

His reasons for using chemicals now are:

☹ To escape
☹ To avoid responsibility
☹ To avoid problems (many of them caused by his chemical use)

STAGE 4 – USING TO FEEL NORMAL

what does he take?
Drink and drugs are now the only thing Dave can count on to make him feel good. He uses them most days, compulsively – they're uppermost in his mind all the time. He can no longer predict how much he will use or what the outcome will be. Usually he takes everything he's got, even if he'd like to save some for tomorrow. He goes on binges, often staying drunk or high for several days at a time.

how does he behave?
Dave gets very aggressive and takes more risks. He often doesn't realise how 'out of it' he is, and does things that are dangerous. To his family and friends, he seems like a different person. Yet he doesn't believe he has a problem. He is expelled from college, his parents throw him out, even his friends who use drugs 'recreationally' are worried about him.

what's going on inside him?
Dave is out of touch with what's really happening to him. He can always think of someone worse than he is, which he

takes to mean he must be okay. He abandons all the rules he made for himself. Because of his irresistible urge to use chemicals, his life revolves around them – nothing else matters. When he's not drunk or high, he feels paranoid, totally cut off from everyone and everything else, suicidal, full of despair and self-hatred. He has become dependent on chemicals: he feels he MUST use them.

His reasons for continuing now are:

- 😔 To feel 'normal'
- 😔 To avoid emotional pain
- 😔 To avoid withdrawal symptoms
- 😔 To avoid facing up to his problem

The details of each stage of the road to addiction will vary from one individual to another and according to the drugs they are using. But these stages are very common 'landmarks' in the development of addiction. In the next chapter, four people talk about their experiences. See if you can spot the different stages.

note

I   This model was first used by Dr Vernon E Johnson, founder of the Johnson Institute, Minnesota, USA.

4 THE HIGH LIFE
True-life stories

ROSIE
• • • • • • •

Even as a child I used things like sweets, possessions and friends as a comfort, to try and fill the emptiness inside myself. I started smoking pot when I was sixteen, which got me mixing with drug users. My parents were very strict and, when I suddenly had more freedom by getting married at the age of eighteen, I abused it. The first time I used Speed, I thought I'd found the key to everything. It seemed this was what I'd been looking for all my life. I was a bit low afterwards, but the memory of that good feeling didn't ever leave me. Because I'm an extreme person, I then threw myself into that lifestyle – endless parties, raves, having a fantastic time. As a child I'd only felt loved and accepted when everything was great – when my bedroom was tidy, when everything was under control – and I think I chose my particular drugs (Speed, Ecstasy, cocaine) because that's how they made me feel. I was always on top form.

I was able to sustain that lifestyle for a while, then I started to leap-frog from one drug-taking time to another. Using drugs really is a slippery slope, but you don't realise it because you're having so much fun and all your friends are doing it. Friends who take drugs together usually feel there is a very strong bond between them. I thought we'd die for each other. I felt great when I'd just taken drugs, but then crap afterwards. Looking back, I think I turned from experimenting to becoming an addict when I started chasing that good feeling because I couldn't bear to be without it. I didn't feel I had a problem. I wasn't out of my face all the time – I was just getting rid of the fear and dread. Breakfast would be orange juice with Speed in it.

Things started falling apart. My marriage ended. I asked my mum to babysit my daughter, and then didn't go back for eleven months. I didn't want my daughter because she got in the way of my partying. I was completely blinkered – I truly thought it was all under control. My drug use kept increasing. It felt so bad coming back to reality that I always took more drugs to escape again.

My boyfriend and I decided that if we moved abroad we would be able to give up drugs. As if! The lies you tell yourself are unbelievable. When you're out of your head, you can put the whole world to rights: but once you're coming down, the only thing you can think about is how you'll get your next fix. Instead of giving up, we started trafficking drugs. We were ripping all our friends off by mixing the drugs with whatever else we had around, so that we'd earn more money. There was me thinking, *My mates, I'd die for them*, and I was probably killing them by giving them Ajax!

Life consisted of flash cars, parties, hotels, frequent trips abroad – we were in the fast lane! But I was starting to realise I'd lost control. I was waking up unable to remember the night before or how I'd got wherever I was. I couldn't recapture the good feeling I'd first had. So I took more and more, which would knock me unconscious. I lost a lot of weight, my hair was falling out, my teeth were loose in my gums, I'd wee blood after a weekend raving because my kidneys were damaged. When I was coming down I'd hallucinate, so I took more to get rid of the hallucinations. I took anything and everything, wanting to see what effect it would have. The only thing I wouldn't take was heroin. I took tablets with heroin in them, but I wouldn't take heroin powder because that would have made me a 'junkie'. Can you believe it! I lied all the time and believed my lies myself.

I didn't want to take drugs any more. Where I'd once craved to feel good, I now craved to feel normal. When I was using, I was still the life and soul of the party. But when I wasn't, I was like a frightened little mouse, too scared even to open the door. I wanted to die. I thought about suicide for a long time, and eventually took an overdose. I did want to die, but God was at work!

I had never thought about God before. The only time I'd used the word was when I had my head down the toilet. But in hospital I picked up a Bible and opened it at Psalm 116. I thought, *Shit, this is me.* It described exactly how I felt. I realised that there was someone who didn't care what I looked like or how cool I was, someone who really did love me and who would help me. I remember crying out to him, saying, 'I've tried everything, I'm totally broken.' For the first time, I realised there was a way out. This was a major turning point – finding God ruined my drug-taking. After that, I never had the same good experiences from drugs. I tried to leave them alone completely, but started using them in binges. I would go to church and come home feeling great. I knew there was a God who loved me, but didn't grasp it was unconditional. So every time I blew it I'd think, *That's it, I may as well continue now,* and go on a massive binge. Every time I eventually came back, I felt God smile at me, like I was his child.

I took a long time to learn. I'd binge, then come back, binge, then come back. It used to take me all the time I was straight to clear up the devastation I'd caused. I'd wake up in police cells, not knowing how I got there or where my child was. Cocaine made me vicious. One time I was coming down after using all weekend, and was invited out to dinner with my parents. The waitress upset me, so I attacked her with a fork in the middle of the restaurant. My poor family were thrown out, leaving this waitress bleeding on the floor. Another time, I spent eleven hours in a police cell after attacking my house-mate with a hammer. Mad, mad, behaviour. But that madness had become normal. Even though I moved to a new area, to try to break away from my boyfriend and drugs, I still migrated towards drug users, because I felt secure in the familiarity of that scene.

Whenever I took drugs again, I felt awful and cried out to God. One time I felt him say to me, 'Why do you only call me in times of need? You've got to follow me, not just call on me in trouble. Otherwise you'll carry on in this state forever.' Gradually there were longer gaps between binges. But whenever I felt stable for a while, I tended to turn away from God and go back to what I knew. It felt safer to go back to feelings that were familiar than to have feelings I'd never had before – remorse, sadness, joy, love.

You're so focused on yourself that you forget about the people around you, and only since stopping have I realised the devastation I caused. My father has said to me that he felt totally helpless. Towards the end, my parents stopped giving me money and eventually washed their hands of me. I was very bitter about that for a long time, but my father told me they did it for their own protection. He was sure a policeman would come and tell them I was dead at any moment. In fact, stopping giving me money and looking after me probably helped me get to the point where I was determined to give up. My daughter used to have terrible nightmares. She would pull her hair out, colour me in with felt-tip when I was lying unconscious on the floor. And I still thought I was a good mother! At four, she was a little adult. Physically, I've done myself lasting damage. My memory isn't so good, and when I'm very tired I get mild flashbacks, which is a sign of brain damage. I get pains in my joints, which I think is from dancing hour after hour when my body was very run-down.

At first I wondered how God could ever sort out the total mess my life was in. It's been gradual, but when I look back like this I realise things have been sorted out. Life today isn't a bed of roses, but I don't have to be out of my face. There are still times when I feel down, but I now have the most amazing family, a wonderful husband, and friends I treasure. I *love* my husband and children, whereas before I only loved things I could put up my nose or down my throat. I would have settled for much less, and I thank God for it all, because I know it's God-given.

Rosie and Rebecca are both in their late twenties and had used drugs over a ten-year period. Now let's hear from people still in their teens.

Bryan

I'm nineteen, and I've already spent a total of two and a half years in prison because of my drinking. The last time I was out I only lasted a week, which was pretty devastating because I hadn't drunk for several months and I thought this meant I'd have it under control again.

There have been plenty of times in prison when I've said to myself I won't drink any more, but as soon as I'm out it's straight to that off-licence or to the pub. It starts off slow, but before I know it I'm back to being drunk most days. Because alcohol is all around me, part of everyday life, I find it too hard to resist.

At first I didn't like the taste of alcohol, but I made myself get used to it so that I could drink like everyone else. By thirteen I started drinking a lot. I'd get other people to buy it for me. As I got older, I needed more and more to get the same buzz. I started drinking spirits and eventually got through a couple of bottles a day. It was making me so ill – when I woke up in the morning, I would feel really sick and couldn't eat or do a thing until I'd had another drink, to get rid of the withdrawals.

I suppose by the time I was sixteen drink had control of my life: I gave up other interests; I couldn't get a job; all my relationships with girlfriends broke up. One time I tried to cross a dual carriageway while I was drunk, and I was hit by a car and broke my leg. In the end there wasn't anything in my life except drink and hanging around with other drinkers.

My problem is that if it's there I'll drink it, and I don't stop until I black out. I've tried to control it – just have one or two – but I always end up drunk. By that stage I've no idea what's going on and what I'm doing. I've woken up in police stations many times and had no idea how I got there or what I'd done wrong. I've been in prison for burglaries I don't remember doing because I was too drunk (no wonder I got caught!) and for joining in the rioting in Trafalgar Square after the England v Germany European Cup match in 1995 (also while very drunk!). A week after the last time I was released, I was back in for violent offences, which again I can hardly remember. I think I realised I had a problem, but when you're drinking you don't care. My mum always told me I drank too much, but I took no notice. I thought I was in control – which I wasn't at all.

I feel really stupid. I've let myself and my family down. In a way it's a relief to be back in prison because it means I can't drink and so I can't do any more damage. It seems inevitable I'll keep coming back here – past experience tells me that if I drink I'll soon be in big trouble again, and I can't imagine that I'll ever be able to leave alcohol alone. I've tried but I always give in, because everyone around me is drinking. I don't think about the future or have any dreams or aspirations. It all seems hopeless really.

ANDY
● ● ● ● ● ● ●

Drugs were something new and exciting for me to try. They went with my personality – I'm sociable and have always taken risks. I felt I had a reputation to live up to – people looked up to me. And because they assumed I would have tried drugs, I thought I'd better! I'm 18 now, but I've been smoking dope since I was about 12, and tried LSD. Then, when I was 16, I started taking Ecstasy and Speed at home with friends. At 17 my use really increased. At first I enjoyed all of it, even the 'come down', because it made me feel I was at the cutting edge of things. I loved dancing, the music and socialising while using drugs. I thought it broke down barriers between people, gave you something in common.

I am an ambitious person with clear goals for the future, but I found myself slowly losing sight of these. My sights became fixed only on the next opportunity to have a good time taking drugs and being with like-minded people. My 'daily life' began to revolve around drugs – getting enough money, getting the drugs organised – along with the people and places to go. On the occasions that it all failed, I felt as though the world had come to an end. I didn't realise what the cause was at the time, but taking Speed began to make me extremely self-conscious. I'd been a confident person, but I became convinced people didn't like me. I would get really paranoid if they didn't talk to me. I also became aware that a lot of the time I was spouting absolute rubbish when I spoke. No wonder I got paranoid about no one wanting to talk to me – it was true!

After a while I didn't have a long enough time between bouts of drug-taking to come back to reality. I didn't think the problem was that bad, because I knew lots of people in a much worse state than me and that comforted me. I had blinkers over my eyes, concentrating only on the next drug-related event. I wanted to lift the haze I'd created, but I didn't know how to. I didn't want to believe drugs were the cause of the problem. They seemed to have too much fun attached to them, fun I wouldn't find anywhere else. I got really confused. My thinking powers and ability to assess problems were being eroded by the drugs. Confusion ran wild.

As time gaps began to shorten between events, I just couldn't cope with all the depression and frustration that followed the good times. I started taking cocaine during the week to try and get rid of the lows. It felt like my soul was being eaten away. I lost a lot of weight, and started to get various health problems because my body was so run-down. I spent all my £1,200 savings on drugs. I became so frustrated at not being able to help myself and at the loss of the person I had been.

I'd never borrowed money off anyone, and took pride in being able to help my mum out from time to time. So it was the final straw when I borrowed money for drugs – off my mum. A few days later I crashed my car – a classic I was really proud of –

while driving the 'morning after the night before'. It crossed my mind that the accident was God trying to get through to me, but I didn't know anything about him. The one Christian I was friendly with, Neil, helped me begin to see that there was much more to life. But more about that later.

EMMA
••••••••

I was born in 1980, on Merseyside. I had lots of friends and a secure, happy life. At senior school I achieved good marks and was always top of the class. Things were going really well.

Shortly after my thirteenth birthday, I made some new friends and started to hang around the local park, drinking and smoking and having a good time. Before long I tried cannabis and Acid, just to see what would happen, and I liked the effects. I started to smoke pot more and more. I began skipping school and falling out with my mum and step-dad, but that didn't stop me – I was having a good time and I wasn't giving it up for anyone. After a while I built up a tolerance for pot and needed something stronger. That was when I was introduced to heroin.

I started hanging around the house of a girl who was much older than me. We all knew she took heroin, but we didn't take much notice. Her house was just somewhere to get away from parents and to smoke pot! She'd offered me heroin a few times, but no way was I going to take it! That was a loser's game and I wasn't going to play it. But the more time I spent there, the more curious I became. I really wanted to feel the way all the smack-heads felt – they looked so content and happy when they were high. If only I had seen them withdrawing, I would probably never have tried it myself.

The first time I smoked heroin, I was scared and excited. The feeling it left me with was great. Because it was the summer holidays and I wasn't at school, I spent more and more time at this house where I thought I'd discovered the meaning of life! Everyone who drifted in and out would give me some of their heroin, and because I didn't need much I would be stoned all day. It was no hassle getting it, so I didn't realise how addicted I was becoming. Then one day I asked one of the guys there for some. Back came the reply – 'No, Emma. We always sort you out. It's about time you sorted *us.*'

I really wanted some gear, but didn't have any money. He said, 'If you need it, sell your ring.' (I was wearing a £200 ring that my boyfriend had bought me.)

'No way would I sell this,' I replied. 'Anyway, I don't need the gear. I can do without.'

Within an hour I would have sold everything I owned for a fix. Sweat was pouring off me; I was shaky, shivering all over. I felt so disorientated and desperate, it was dreadful. I threw the ring at this guy and grabbed hungrily at the £25 worth of gear he gave me in exchange. I smoked it, and within minutes I felt like my old self again. A while later he came back with the £150 worth of heroin he'd bought with my ring. I felt I was entitled to some. He went crazy. 'You owe us, Emma,' he yelled at me, 'so you're not getting any. This isn't a baby's game you're playing, so you better grow up. Now get out!' I felt like a scrap of dirt, and I realised how malicious and selfish drug addicts can be. Now I had no choice but to be the same. I was caught in a trap from which few people ever escape.

Over the next few months I changed from an intelligent, outgoing girl into a vicious, withdrawn, scheming junkie, with nothing on my mind except scoring and fixing. I left home and was dragged back a thousand times by social workers and the police, but I didn't want to be at home. My parents were devastated. They kept telling me they loved me, but because all I could think about was drugs this made me feel smothered and frustrated. My boyfriend and I spent most of our time stealing and selling things to get high. I sold all my jewellery, my CDs and my new stereo. I even sold my clothes and stole from my family. When I had nothing left and nowhere to live, I managed to get us a roof over our heads each night in various junkies' houses, by handling stolen goods. It didn't come cheap – they wanted a lot of drugs – and I worked myself into the ground to get the money. I became a professional shoplifter, stealing in town through the day, and breaking into cars and garden sheds at night. All the police knew me as a thief and a junkie, and I couldn't walk down the street without being stopped and searched.

I became depressed, and this led me deeper into the drug world. I wouldn't have anything to do with my family or my old friends. I was so alone. I had dug my own grave and there was no escaping it. I didn't sleep or eat properly, and my weight dropped from nine and a half stone to five. I was like the walking dead. I didn't wash or wear clean clothes. I was full of pain and emptiness inside. When you're desperate for drugs, you'll do anything to get them.

Nothing can come between a junkie and their fix. I saw many violent fights between addicts, and was even involved in some myself.

I was deeply in love with heroin, and it held onto me so tightly I felt I would never break free. I tried many times, but never managed to last more than 48 hours, and that put me through hell and back. I gave myself to drugs, and the lifestyle that went with it, completely. I was broken and defeated at fourteen years of age. I plodded on through the next few months. My social worker heard of a drug project she thought might be able to help me, but I held little hope. I felt trapped forever. By now I was having difficulty finding enough money, as I was so well known to the police and shop security guards. I was in town one day, penniless and feeling desperate for drugs, when I bumped into another addict. He agreed to sort me out. I near enough ran back to his flat with him! All the equipment used for injecting was laid out ready. 'I don't bang up,' I said, and walked out.

Halfway down the street I turned back. The withdrawals were getting painful and I was desperate for some more. I felt disgusted with myself as I watched him prepare the drugs for injecting. It looked evil, but I was evil, so what difference did it make? 'Roll up your sleeve,' he said. I was past caring. I hardly felt the prick of the needle as the rush of heroin flowed into my bloodstream and I slumped to the floor.

When I came round, I could hardly walk. But I knew I had to get home, as my boyfriend would be waiting for his drugs. I didn't have enough money to buy a pack of cigarettes, let alone a decent fix. By the time

I got there, my withdrawals were on the way back. My boyfriend opened the door, smiling expectantly. 'I haven't scored,' I said, knowing what was coming next. He dragged me in and started beating me up. He demanded that I go and see our regular supplier and beg for drugs. I went, but I had stooped to my very lowest. I was willing to do *anything* to break free.

I was so weak and desperate, I asked for arrangements to be made for me to live with a couple in the south, within 48 hours. I made contact with my family again. My mum was so relieved that I was finally getting help. It was hard for me to leave the town that I'd grown up in, and hard to leave the drugs. I didn't know how I was going to cope, but I was determined.

For the next week I had to fight every step of the way to stop myself giving up, but this time it was a different struggle. The physical withdrawal wasn't too bad, it was the mental withdrawal that was tiring me out. It was like a raging battle going on inside my head, and it took every ounce of energy I had to force myself to think positively.

Then I was invited to go to church. I was sceptical, but agreed to go. Everyone was nice, but I felt they were fakes and were really disgusted at me. I couldn't have been more wrong! They offered to pray for me that night to be healed and restored. I didn't see any blinding flashes of light or anything, but I felt different. And when I got home, I threw the remainder of the methadone I'd been prescribed down the sink. I knew I was going to make it this time and I wasn't on my own anymore. Someone was with me, even though I didn't know who he was at that time.

I spent as much time as I could at church, and a couple of months later I gave my life to Jesus, alone in my bedroom. I knew he loved me and had helped me through a fierce battle. He had fought for me, and I could only repay him by giving myself to him completely. Only through the power of Jesus was I saved from death. Others haven't been so fortunate.

Many people leave their stories there, and it sounds like their lives became perfect the minute they found Jesus. I am not one of those people! I've been clean for fifteen months now, and am back in education. I still struggle with various problems. I have a deep feeling of regret, but also know that God is slowly healing me. I may have an amazing testimony, and you may even be wishing yours was as exciting as mine. But please hear me when I say that I'm still suffering the consequences and I wish that, like thousands of Christian teenagers, I could have a simple yet special story to tell instead of the horrific one I have just shared with you.

Some people may say that these stories don't give a balanced picture, that they are all extreme cases. Well, Andy is typical of thousands of people involved in the club scene. In the course of my work with addicts, I do tend to meet extreme cases – not many people kill their babies after using cannabis. BUT THESE PEOPLE NEVER THOUGHT THEY'D END UP LIKE THAT. They intended to be just like everyone else. Then one day they woke up and realised something had happened. They had gone over the edge. They had become an extreme case.

⑤ SUSSED
Understanding who we are

'Why do I always feel so down, that only drugs and alcohol make me feel better?' *(Church leader's 16-year-old daughter)*

To get the most out of life and avoid being sidetracked by drugs or anything else, we need to understand who we are and why we're here. This chapter will explore the first of these questions.

The search for identity

As we get older, we start trying to work out who we are as an individual separate from everyone else. Often we focus on what we look like, but our identity is much more than that. What we look like, what we own, who our friends are – all these are to do with image. Our identity is who we are on the inside. It involves what we believe, what we like doing, what we think is important. These things usually change several times during our teens, and we can end up feeling pretty insecure and confused.

BODY, SOUL AND SPIRIT
In our teens we tend to focus on our bodies – particularly what we look like. But an individual isn't just a body: we are soul and spirit too. The soul is that part of us that is centred on the emotions, the mind and the will – our ability to

feel, think and make choices. The spirit is the part that will last for all eternity. To God, our bodies, minds, emotions and spirits are all important, otherwise he wouldn't have given them to us – so why do we waste so much time worrying only about our bodies (particularly when they're the part of us we won't take with us when we die)?

People who don't know God are ruled either by their souls or their bodies. However, when a person becomes a Christian he is transformed and renewed, so that his whole being – body, mind and spirit – becomes able and willing to do what the Holy Spirit says is best (Galatians 5:16; Romans 12:1–2).

Just as our bodies need food to maintain our physical health, our emotions and spirits need 'food' to maintain our emotional and spiritual health. We know when our bodies need more fuel because we feel hungry. In the same way, we 'hunger' for the things we need to stay emotionally and spiritually healthy. Let's look now at what kind of emotional and spiritual food we need.

HAPPINESS IS...

Why did God make human beings? Because the Trinity – the Father, the Son and the Holy Spirit – wanted more opportunities to express OUTWARDLY the love they felt for each other.

In the Bible, God called Abraham and Moses, the two great Israelite leaders, 'My friends'. Imagine that! Being a friend of God! God made humankind so that we could have a relationship with him and know his love. A big part of that friendship is communication, and this is two-way: people talk to God, and he shares his thoughts and feelings with them. He involves people in carrying out his plans for the world. He could do it all himself, but he wants us to play a part.

Imagine – a computer is won in a raffle by someone who has no idea what it is. The winner is thrilled – because it will make the perfect plant-stand! A few years on, she would say that the computer has done pretty well. It's been very useful and of tremendous value in showing off her house plants. But anyone who knows what a computer really is and what it could have been used for would feel that this person having it has been a total waste. In the same way, if we live independently of God, we'll miss out on the whole reason why we're here. Rebecca described how she had tried one thing after another, but had always felt that something was missing. That's because something was!

In the first century, Paul the apostle told the Christians at Ephesus:

> Long before [God] laid down earth's foundations, he had us in mind, had settled on us as the focus of his love, to be made whole and holy by his love. Long, long ago he decided to adopt us into his family through Jesus Christ. (What pleasure he took in planning this!)…
>
> Because of the sacrifice of the Messiah, his blood poured out on the altar of the Cross, we're a free people – free of penalties and punishments chalked up by all our misdeeds. And not just barely free, either. *Abundantly* free! He thought of everything, provided for everything we could possibly need, letting us in on the plans he took such delight in making. He set it all out before us in Christ, a long-range plan in which everything would be brought together and summed up in him, everything in deepest heaven, everything on planet earth.
>
> It's in Christ that we find out who we are and what we are living for. Long before we first heard of Christ and got our hopes up, he had his eye on us, had

designs on us for glorious living, part of the overall purpose he is working out in everything and everyone. *(Ephesians 1, from The Message by Eugene H Peterson, NavPress Publishing Group [US], 1994)*

God has designed us so that we can only truly be fulfilled when we are living in a 'full on' friendship with him. Anything else is second best.

ME AND MY MATES

During our teens, we are discovering who we are in relation to other people. God designed us so that what it means to be 'us' is only fully expressed when we relate to others. An eyeball on a dissection plate may be very interesting, but we can only really appreciate what it is when it is connected to a body and doing its job:

> 'We are like the various parts of a human body. Each part gets its meaning from the body as a whole, not the other way around. The body we're talking about is Christ's body of chosen people. Each of us finds our meaning and function as a part of his body. But as a chopped-off finger or cut-off toe we wouldn't amount to much, would we? So since we find ourselves fashioned into all these excellently formed and marvellously functioning parts in Christ's body, let's just go ahead and be what we were made to be, without enviously or pridefully comparing ourselves with each other, or trying to be something we aren't.' *(Romans 12, The Message)*

God with us
●●●●●●●●●●●●●

A friend told me recently about a letter she had once written. Here's what she said:

When my son was 13, he was extremely unhappy at school. He became the target of a lot of bullying, and all his friends deserted him. One day I had to go into the school to fetch him because he was unwell. There I 'saw' and 'felt' his acute loneliness. I decided to write a letter to him, telling him what I somehow could not verbalise face to face – how sad I was for his deep unhappiness. And I expressed the desire to go *with* him to school, if that were possible.

Of course, I knew it wasn't and would, in fact, have set up even more difficulties for him. But the fact was that I longed to give him the benefit of my company. I wanted to be there, so that when he was lonely he could turn to me, and I could support him and help him through. He wouldn't be alone and friendless. The simple truth was that I loved him dearly. His hurt and pain hurt me, and I wanted to be with him in it.

e e e
············

My friend's feelings express just a tiny measure of God's love and concern for us. He hasn't just abandoned us to cope with life the best we can. He wants to be with us in it. However, unlike that mother, God can get alongside us and help us in everything we go through. Because Jesus became a human being, and was rejected and betrayed, he understands all that we feel.

THE MAIN MAN

God has designed human beings so that we all have three emotional and spiritual needs deep down inside. These are for:[1]

1 **Security and unconditional love** – a feeling of belonging, and having people who will love us no matter what.
2 **Significance and impact** – knowing that we have got something to contribute, that we can have a purpose in life.
3 **Self-worth** – a sense of being valued.

These three deep needs influence our emotions and behaviour most of the time.

Imagine there are tanks labelled 'Love', 'Significance' and 'Self-worth' inside each of us. During childhood these are usually kept filled by our parents and, because they are full, we aren't even aware that they exist. Sometimes they're NOT kept full, so an individual may grow up feeling unloved and insignificant. No one wants to feel like this for long, so people find ways to make themselves feel better, as Rosie did by using food and possessions.

As we get into our teens, we realise that the world is much more complex than it used to seem. Adults start having higher expectations of us, and people may not appear to love us as much as they used to. Being cute may have worked when you were six. But when you're sixteen, skipping around wearing your fairy outfit doesn't have quite the same effect (especially if you're a boy)! The things that made us feel significant or valued when we were little also stop working. For example, someone who felt special because they were top of the class at junior school, can be totally lost when they move on to secondary school.

When our childhood ways of keeping those tanks full stop working, we start to feel insecure, unimportant, worthless. Not nice, right? So we look for ways to get rid of those feelings. Addictive behaviour – whether it be addiction to drugs, sex, food or work – is one of the roads people may go down in order to escape them. It may make them feel better for a while, but what we all really need is a way to fill the tanks up again. It's as though we are trying to answer these questions:

? What kind of person must I be to belong and to be loved?
? What kind of person must I be to have an impact on the world?
? What kind of person must I be to be worth something?

At first, most people try to make their old ways work. If this fails, they become angry, frightened and confused. Some turn to rebellious or self-destructive behaviour because they lose hope of ever finding ANYTHING that will work.

Often people assume that there must be something wrong with them which is causing others not to love or value them as much as they need. They try to figure out what this is so that they can change, and the tendency is to focus on their physical appearance. Many become desperately self-conscious, thinking that the whole world immediately notices their most hideous features. If only this or that were different, people would like them more. So they change their image in the hope that this will happen. But then they find that they can't let others get too close, in case they discover the reality behind the image.

By their late teens people have usually found ways to feel loved, important and valued which they think work reasonably well. These could include having boyfriends/girlfriends, a career or material possessions, or engaging in rebellious or criminal behaviour. But are these things guaranteed to work? What can go wrong?

God designed us so that true and reliable security, significance and self-worth only come from our relationship with him. All through history the devil has tricked us into thinking that this isn't true, that other things are better than relying on God. So we wander off, trying these things to see if they will do what only God can.

true love

Only God can love us unconditionally. He doesn't have ulterior motives or 'bad' days when he'd rather not speak to anybody. Jesus was willing to give up his life so that we could be adopted into God's family, so he isn't suddenly going to reject us, is he?

true significance

Recently I read about a man called James Robison, who had endured an awful start in life. His mother was an orphan who was later abandoned, penniless, by her husband. One night she was raped and became pregnant as a result. Abortion was still illegal, so she decided to kill herself. She cried out to God in desperation, and heard him say, 'Have this baby. It will bring joy to the world.'

For years there was no sign of this happening! His mother nearly died giving birth to him and, because she was so poor, he spent much of his childhood with foster parents. James was painfully shy and showed no potential for anything. Then one night, when he was in his late teens, he felt God call him to preach. No one else agreed this could be possible. The following week at work, in the middle of his lunch-break, he was overcome with a sense of God's heart for his work mates, and started telling them about Jesus. Since then James has helped millions of people get to know Jesus.[2]

James Robison probably felt totally worthless and insignificant when he was growing up. He wasn't even meant to be here. Yet all the things that were stacked against him became irrelevant because GOD knew him. God had a plan for his life and would equip him to fulfil it. Could this be true for other people too?

God knows you. Doesn't that make you significant? He has given you a unique personality and talents. There is a contribution that you alone can make to life. If you don't make it, no one else will. We need to realise just how much influence for good or bad we have on others all the time. There is an enormous, 'life-and-death' purpose to our lives, and we need to grasp this when we're young so that we don't waste any time.

true self-worth

We only appreciate our real value when we know what God says we are worth. Our opinions about ourselves are formed while we are growing up, particularly by how we are treated by people who matter to us, and by the way we think others see us. We may end up feeling that we're not worth anything, but God says we are of great value. What he says is true. Real healing will come from listening to him.

If you don't like yourself, try to work out what made you feel this way. Ask someone to pray with you for God to heal the things that have caused you to have such a poor view of yourself. Ask for a revelation of God's love. Believing in our heads isn't enough – we need the Holy Spirit to reveal it to our hearts. Meditate on Psalm 139, and use it to start replacing your old thoughts about yourself with what God says about you. Sometimes we don't like ourselves because there's a big gap between what we think we should be like and what we really ARE like. We need ideals to work towards. But we must also remember that God loves us totally TODAY, and won't love us any more even if we become perfect (which we won't!).

Trying to satisfy our three deep needs with things other than God is idolatry and independence, ie it is sinful. It is also silly! God explains it like this:

> 'My people have committed two sins: They have forsaken me, the spring of living water, and have dug their own cisterns, broken cisterns that cannot hold water.' *(Jeremiah 2:13, New International Version)*

God is the spring of pure, life-giving water, and everything else is like dirty water from an animal trough. Yet we prefer to drink from the trough instead of savouring the best thing around. Jesus tells us, 'Whoever drinks the water I give will not thirst again.' But we say, 'No thanks, I'd rather try a few muddy troughs first. I'll come back to you if they don't work.'

But deep down we are all rebellious. We don't like admitting that we need God totally and utterly – we want to feel independent. The devil tells us that those troughs are more satisfying than God – the spring of living water. And he makes sure that the water in the troughs DOES taste nice at first, to lure us into carrying on drinking it. So, a lot of the time, sin is enjoyable. (It may leave us feeling 'Yuck' afterwards, but it usually feels great at the time.) If sin wasn't fun, it wouldn't have any appeal, would it? That's how a trap works – if you were a mouse, would you be tempted into one where the goodie on offer was a mouldy tea bag? Rebecca described how she fell for that lie and thought that living away from God had more to offer. She tried clubbing, career, travel, drugs, romance and other religions in her search for purpose and satisfaction. In the end, she discovered that only God could satisfy her deep-down thirst.

We are designed to feel passionate about God. Spiritual passion is about wanting something deeply, with all our being; it's about having something worth living for and worth dying for. The Bible puts it this way:

Love the Lord your God with all your heart and with all your soul and with all your strength.' *(Deuteronomy 6:5, NIV)*

That's passion!

Most people never direct this sort of energy towards God. In fact, they will direct it towards just about anything else. But he has designed us so that the more we experience of him, the more we will want. Doesn't this sound rather like what people describe when they take drugs?

The fact is that the devil sidetracks the passion meant for God into sensual experiences, and attaching spiritual passion to the wrong things can make it seem like those things control us. When we look at life like this, drug use may not seem any more 'wrong' than any of the other ways people try to meet their three deep needs (although drug use obviously can do more damage than some things). God is more interested in what is going on inside us. He wants us to receive our sense of being loved and valued from him, and then to serve him and others out of what he gives us.

Getting emotional

Some Christians seem to think it's wrong to have emotions. This is rubbish! God has emotions: the Bible shows him feeling angry, joyful, sad. Jesus cried and got angry. Your emotions are part of who you are. If you bury them, you end up not being fully yourself.

Advertising suggests that we should always feel good. 'Use this shampoo – wear this – and you'll always feel great!' You get it in churches too! But how can we possibly expect to feel great all the time when we live in a world full of sickness, injustice and evil? If you believe that you shouldn't have 'bad' feelings, you end up burying them or pretending they're not there.

Imagine a house with a cellar. The owners are very respectable and think that putting their rubbish out for the binmen would spoil their image. They don't want anyone to know they have nasty things like rubbish, so they chuck it in the cellar. The bags are soon all rotting away and start to stink the house out. The cellar is crammed full. Every now and then the cellar door bursts open, but the house-owners shove the rubbish back in again before anyone notices. One day there's no room left. Then what? Wouldn't it have been better to put the rubbish out for the binmen each week?

I was like that. I didn't know how to cope with feeling hurt, so I shoved lots of pain down inside. When I became a Christian, I got the impression from somewhere that you were a failure if you ever felt down or upset. So I pretended I wasn't! All the emotions in the cellar made me depressed, and in the end I had to spend years clearing it out – with God's help. Clearing out the rubbish of buried emotions is a lot more unpleasant after it's been rotting inside us for a few years than if we had dealt with our problems as they arose and allowed Jesus to help us through them! One day a crisis is sure to come which will force us to face up to them. Why put it off? We need to follow Jesus' example – he poured out how he felt to God.

We too can be real with God. Often we think, *But I shouldn't feel like this*, but the fact is we do and God knows that we do. So why pretend? It only drives us away from God, away from other people and away from reality. Christians should be able to live in reality more than anyone, yet churches are full of people pretending. I can't stand it!

We often feel the way we do because we have tried and failed to meet our three deep needs independently of God.

If we talk to God, he can help us deal with the causes of how we are feeling and show us how to view things differently. The trouble is, when we're going through a rough patch we often run away from God and look elsewhere for comfort and for answers. Rebecca described how alcohol and drugs helped her bury her grief when her mum died. This just meant that the grief was stored away and had to be faced years later. Things like drugs and alcohol do numb painful feelings for a little while, but they stop you from learning to cope with difficult situations and emotions, which is part of growing up. The only real way out is to work through them – and you can do this, with God's help.

Where do drugs and alcohol fit in?

In the following list, circle any of the feelings you have had in the past week.

afraid angry anxious bored confused confident disappointed embarrassed excited frustrated furious guilty happy hopeless hurt inadequate insecure jealous lonely loved nervous peaceful powerful powerless proud rejected sad safe scared shy stressed tense unloved wanted worthless worthwhile

Sometimes when people keep having the same uncomfortable feelings and don't know how to handle them, they resort to drugs or alcohol to get rid of them. If they get into the habit of doing this, they become unable to cope with normal life without chemicals, unable to admit or express their true feelings. Eventually they lose touch with their true selves, and they lose touch with God and other people.

I was terribly shy when I was younger. Alcohol would have

helped me to feel confident whenever I socialised. But I felt the real solution was to keep asking God to deal with the causes of my shyness, so that I could genuinely feel more confident. The alcohol 'solution' would have been short-changing myself. God has brought me a long way since then.

Which of the uncomfortable feelings you circled do you have most often? Have you ever used drugs or alcohol to change those feelings? What happened? Can you ask some-one to help you find a better way to handle them?

To wrap it up

We find out who we really are in the context of our rela-tionship with God and with other people. Don't waste time wishing you were more like someone else. God made you YOU for a reason. No one else can develop the potential he has given you. So go on – be yourself to the full!

notes

1   This concept was first described by Dr L Crabb in
    Basic Principles of Biblical Counselling, Zondervan, 1975.
    Since then it has been adapted and developed by
    many people, including me!

2   I read this story in *Surprised by the Voice of God*, Jack
    Deere, Kingsway, 1996.

6 UNDER THE INFLUENCE

Handling the culture we live in

In the last chapter, we looked at how what goes on inside us can influence the way we behave. Now let's see what else may influence the choices we make.

Whenever I talk about things like peer pressure or the influence of the media, people get offended. They assume that I'm implying they can't think for themselves. Rest assured — I do know you can make your own decisions. You wouldn't stick your head in the fire just because your mate did, right? But some things influence us so subtly, we don't realise it.

The media

Recently, the number of young people who smoke increased following advertising campaigns aimed at their age group. Coincidence? How much do you think the media influences your decisions, your idea of who you are and what you go for in life?

'We don't influence 11–14 year-olds, we own them.'
(*MTV director*)

How can someone else think he has so much power to shape my life that it's like owning me? I don't want to be 'owned' by anyone except God!

Even as Christians, do we allow the media greater influence over us than the Holy Spirit? Instead of letting the Holy

Spirit change us from the inside out, are we altering our image to fit with what the media implies we should be like?

Culture
●●●●●●●●●

In Britain, young people pick up from somewhere the belief that to be cool you must appear independent and mature, be admired by your peers and be seen to be having fun. No one ever spells it out like that, but somehow we take cultural values like this on board without realising it. Can you think of some of the things people do in order to meet these 'image' requirements? Using alcohol, tobacco or drugs may be among them.

'Youth culture' in particular is shaped by the music and fashion industries. We would have to be living on Mars not to be affected! The bands and cult figures around us present an image that suggests they've got all the answers, so when they write songs that imply sex, drugs and all the rest are the way to be happy, it's hard not to be taken in.

Being influenced by our culture isn't wrong. In fact, it's vital that we are. Jesus fitted into the time and place in which he lived. In fact, he looked and behaved so much like everyone else that a lot of people couldn't believe he was anything other than the local carpenter. In many ways, he seemed pretty normal. Yet he was radically different in how he treated people, in what he taught and in the total integrity of his lifestyle (he never sinned). He lived within his culture without being controlled by it. And that's what we should aim for – to live within our culture pretty much like other people, but without allowing ALL our thinking and behaviour to be shaped by it.

This is a balancing act! How far should we take it? The apostle Paul said that he became 'all things to all men' in order to win them for Christ (1 Corinthians 9:22). But does this mean that it's okay to take drugs with a group of people who aren't Christians in order to show them that God wants to be involved in their lives?

Christians have to make Christianity as accessible as possible without doing anything that would contradict any of God's principles. If we do everything our friends do in our attempts to make the gospel relevant to them, we're taking the responsibility for getting through to them away from God and onto ourselves. Sticking to God's standards won't stop him from working in any situation.

How are we to decide which parts of our culture we should go along with and which parts we should ignore? Most aspects of culture are neutral, neither right nor wrong. However, there are things that do run counter to God's standards, and these are the parts we must not take on board. We can sort them out from the rest by testing to see whether they go directly against what Jesus stood for or what the Bible says is true.

Friends
• • • • • • • • •

In our teens, friendships become more important. Having a group of friends is part of fulfilling our desire to belong and to have significance. Identifying with other people helps us to work out who we are.

The only problem is that this identification often concentrates on our outward appearance, our image. But it's who we are inside that really matters. Belonging to a group where everyone's trying to be the same can become restrictive and prevent us from being ourselves. This applies to Christians too. Following Jesus doesn't mean you have to become a clone of the most nerdy person you've ever met (or even of your ultra-cool youth leader)! Following Jesus sets you free to be totally you and totally unlike anyone else.

Role models
•••••••••••••••

While we're working out who we are, we need role models (people we want to imitate) and ideals (standards we want to measure up to). However, we need to be careful what role models we choose.

> 'It's extremely important to have someone you can be totally honest with. When I was 18, I had no one, so I turned to David Bowie (!) whose songs were about feelings I was having. He seemed to be the only one who understood me, so his lyrics became very important to me. They offered alternative answers in drugs, 'different' sexual behaviour, being a bit insane. He was my role model for a while. Whoops – look what happened!' *(Rebecca)*

One way having a role model can help is if you ask someone to support and guide you as you move forward with God. Choose someone you like, who is the same sex as you, who is ahead of you in their walk with God, and whose character and lifestyle reflect their integrity. It should be someone who will be totally honest with you. From the start, you both need to be clear about what you're trying to achieve. Don't relate exclusively to your role model – this can lead to problems. Develop other in-depth relationships too.

The apostle Paul was the role model for Timothy, a young church leader, guiding and encouraging him through the problems he faced running a church. Paul didn't have any qualms about telling Timothy to copy him in some of the ways he did things. This sounds like a contradiction of what I said before, about being ourselves, doesn't it? But we don't have to become a carbon copy of someone's whole personality: we need only follow their example, seeing where they have become more like Jesus, how they have overcome a particular sin or learnt to use a particular gift.

Choosing what we're influenced by

How do we make sure that we're influenced more by God than by the people around us, without feeling like we're turning into aliens? The first step is to remember that you are unique and God wants you that way. It's a terrible waste to abandon what he's given you just so you can be more like someone else.

It's what's going on inside us – our three deep needs – that allows outside things to influence us. If we didn't need to be loved, to feel important or valued, we wouldn't care nearly so much about what other people think, would we? I know that in your teens pursuing God is often the hardest option, but it's the only one that really works! Only God can give us true love, true significance and a true sense of our worth.

Remember, Jesus wants to get alongside us in whatever we go through. He could have come to earth looking like Christian Slater or Tom Cruise. Instead he chose to look ordinary, to be rejected and betrayed. Whatever kind of rejection we go through, Jesus has been there first and can help us. He has been a teenager, so he can help us handle the grief!

Unless God feels real to us, our culture is bound to have more impact on us than he does. Allowing ourselves to be constantly filled with the Holy Spirit is vital if we're to be shaped more by God from the inside than by wrong aspects of our culture from the outside. The Holy Spirit will make us strong so that the pressures we face won't bend us and shape us as much as they could do. Many of our decisions are based on fear – fear of ridicule, rejection, the future. But the Holy Spirit makes us bold inside. He lets us know deep down that our lives are safe in God's hands, so we don't need to be afraid.

Exploring God's word will also shape you from the inside. Read the Bible expecting to hear God speak to you as you do so. Think carefully about what you have read, asking him to show you what it means for your life. Isn't it better to be shaped by God's word than by anyone else's?

If there's something missing in your life, if your friends seem to be having a better time than you are, don't write Christianity off. Don't discard God because the religion around him seems about as appealing as a cold bath! Christianity was never meant to be boring. You need to ditch the old bath-water and fill the bath with some deliciously hot water that's a pleasure to jump into. There's a big difference between believing in God and believing him. If we believe God, and act on what he says, life will start hotting up. No longer will we be sitting in lukewarm bath-water!

Dealing with temptation

Temptation to sin comes from three sources: the culture we live in ('the world'); our bodies, minds and emotions (the Bible calls these 'the flesh', 'our sinful nature' or 'the old man'); and, occasionally, direct demonic attack ('the devil').

1 John 2:15–17 describes how temptation comes through culture:

'Don't love the world's ways. Don't love the world's goods. Love of the world squeezes out love for the

Father. Practically everything that goes on in the world – wanting your own way, wanting everything for yourself, wanting to appear important – has nothing to do with the Father. It just isolates you from him. The world and all its wanting, wanting, wanting, is on the way out – but whoever does what God wants is set for eternity.' *(The Message)*

Galatians 5:16–21 describes how we can be tempted by our sinful nature:

'Live by the spirit and you will not gratify the desires of the sinful nature. For the sinful nature desires what is contrary to the Spirit…' *(NIV)*

Galatians lists the things that the sinful human nature likes, such as rage, jealousy, getting drunk and having sex with people we're not married to. Instead of giving in to these desires, we should allow the Spirit within us to produce in our character things like kindness, self-control and patience.

'A man reaps what he sows. The one who sows to please his sinful nature, from that nature will reap destruction…' *(Galatians 6:7–8, NIV)*

The more you give in to a desire to do something wrong, the harder it will be to resist that desire next time. If you do something you shouldn't 'just once, to find out what its like', you are 'sowing to please the sinful nature'. You'll probably want to do it again. Some people find that when they have given something like smoking a foothold, they have to fight the temptation to smoke for years afterwards.

Temptation is a part of life – even Jesus was tempted to sin. But we don't have to give in to it. If you're a Christian, Jesus has set you free from the power of your sinful nature, so you have a choice. When you are being tempted, remind yourself of this! Then focus on God rather than on whatever it is you're trying not to do.

Don't put yourself in situations where you know it will be hard to resist the temptation to do something wrong. If a situation starts to get tricky, make a quick exit! For example, if you know you can't spend time with a certain group of friends without ending up drinking too much, steer clear of the situation.

What should we do when we slip up? Well, remember first that it's okay to change your mind! We often make decisions on impulse and realise later that we have made a mistake. Just because you set off down one road doesn't mean you have to carry on going down it. So, for example, if you're at a party where everyone's getting wrecked, you're drinking yourself and beginning to regret it, you can still stop. There are nearly always 'emergency exits' out of a situation, but we either ignore them or don't notice them because once we have started down a particular route it seems easier to continue.

If you do make a mistake, tell someone so you can work out how to handle the problem differently the next time. But it's no good just talking to a friend who's struggling with the same thing – find someone who can really help.

Don't try to justify what you have done, or you'll be trapped by it. Many people end up taking more drugs or drinking just to get rid of the guilt feelings they have.

If you keep a sin hidden, it will have more of a hold over you. Things tend to lose their power when they're brought out into the open. This will take courage, but it works! So confess what you've done, find God's forgiveness and move on. The devil will probably tell you that you won't be able to go back to God because you're too bad or too much of a failure. But that's a lie designed to rob you of the good things God has for you. God will always want you back!

SAYING 'NO' WITHOUT FEELING STUPID

I've done things I never thought I would do, usually because I wanted to make a good impression on a bloke and going against the flow would have ruined it! Sometimes we think we know what we would or wouldn't do, but get caught out by the circumstances. Imagine yourself in the following scenarios.

You meet your friends at youth group, and they're very giggly. They tell you that they have been sniffing glue round the back, and invite you to join them. How would you feel? What would you do or say? How would the fact they are your friends influence you?

You go with a friend to someone's house to meet up with a group you have never met before. They all start smoking dope. How would you feel? What would you do?

How easy is it to say 'No' to friends as distinct from strangers? Do you think if you say 'Yes' the first time, it will be harder to say 'No' another time?

We always have a choice whether or not to use drugs or alcohol. No one can MAKE us take them. But sometimes, if you don't decide quickly, someone else will decide for you. And if you decide to 'go with the flow', that's like asking someone else to make the decision for you.

It may be easier to say 'No' if you have already thought through your viewpoint. You need to know WHY you don't want to use chemicals. If your only reason for not doing something is because your mum told you not to, you'll look very sad and probably won't last long! You may well find that once people know that for you 'No' means 'No', you're much less likely to be offered drugs.

There are all kinds of ways you can handle a difficult situation. Some are more successful than others! But going against the flow doesn't have to make you seem stuck-up or sad!

In her best-selling book *How to Say No and Keep Your Friends*, Sharon Scott, a counsellor in the US who trains young people internationally, has suggested three steps for making a decision and keeping out of trouble.[1]

1 SIZE UP WHAT'S REALLY GOING ON as soon as you come into a situation. Often we don't see trouble coming. If we can learn to spot it before it hits us, we may be able to avoid it. LOOK to see what's going on before you get involved. Does anything seem suspicious? LISTEN to what people are saying and how they are saying it. ASK YOURSELF, 'IS THIS TROUBLE BREWING?' If it is, keep away!

   The Bible tells us not even to put ourselves in a situation where we're likely to be tempted to do something wrong. Often I think we know very well that a situation is likely to get dodgy. But instead of running away from temptation, we deliberately run towards it. (Or am I the only person who does that?)

2 MAKE A GOOD DECISION. It's easy to get caught up in a situation and forget there may be another side to what's happening. If your friends are excitedly telling you that everyone's going to be there, that there's nothing to worry about and you won't get caught, it's easy to be swept along and forget that actually there may be plenty to worry about and, yes, you could get caught.

   To make a good decision you first need to WEIGH UP THE PROS AND CONS. Ask yourself what are good reasons for doing it, then what are good reasons for not doing it. Then DECIDE whether you want to 'stop or go'. If you don't make a firm decision, your friends will probably keep pressuring you.

3 TAKE ACTION. You need to know what to say and how to say it. Here are ten ways you can get out of a situation without losing face:

> Say 'No' (if you're firm, they'll give up trying to argue)
> Leave the situation
> Ignore what's going on
> Make an excuse and refuse to get involved
> Change the subject
> Make a joke about it
> Act as though you're shocked
> Use flattery
> Suggest a better alternative
> Challenge them about what they're doing

Whether or not these succeed will depend on how you do them. Sound like you mean it, but don't be obnoxious! Don't argue – just refuse to go along, then change the subject or walk away.

Allowing ourselves to be more influenced by God than by these other things won't mean that we become recluses. God wants us to have a positive influence on the people around us, so that we can help to improve things in our particular situation.

note

1 Adapted from *How to Say No and Keep Your Friends* (first edition), written by Sharon Scott, copyright © 1986 (second edition, 1997). Printed by permission of the publisher, HRD Press, Inc, 22 Amherst Road, Amherst, MA 01002, (413) 253-3488, fax (413) 253-3490.

Saying 'no' without feeling stupid

Can get herself out of problem situations, but usually loses a few friends

Can't make up his own mind, so others make it for him

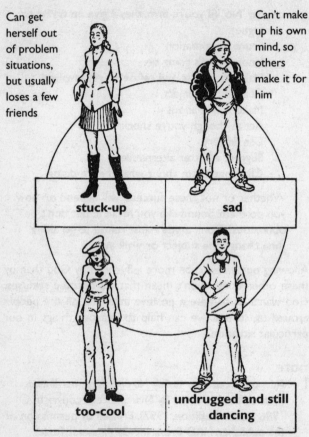

stuck-up

sad

too-cool

undrugged and still dancing

Thinks she can handle it, but ends up putting pressure on herself, trying to live up to her image.

Handles the situation well. Not stuck-up, sad or too-cool. He's staying free and having fun.

7 NOT TO BE SNIFFED AT
What the Bible says

When we look at what the Bible says about addiction, it's important to consider the wider context. Making decisions based on God's word is much bigger than just finding rules on what we can or cannot do.

Why do we need to consider what the Bible says anyway? When you buy a computer, you probably realise that the person who designed it is the person who best understands how it works. So you read the manual to see what this expert has to say. It's the same with us – the one who designed us knows more than anyone how we work. The Bible is the manual he has given us to help us get the best out of our lives.

The Bible gives clear instructions on some things; but other things, like smoking or drugs, aren't even mentioned. Does this mean that God doesn't have any views on these issues?

The Bible was written not to explain 'How' or 'What' (like an encyclopaedia) but 'Why'. It doesn't spell out the answer for every single choice we face; instead it shows us what God is like, why we're alive and why things are the way they are. With that knowledge, we're able to make decisions about a wide variety of things, including those the Bible doesn't specifically mention.

First, let's look at some things that are spelt out.

The use of alcohol

In Bible times people drank alcohol with their meals, rather like we drink tea and coffee today. Jesus obviously thought this was fine: when they ran out of wine at a wedding reception, he created some more out of water (John 2:1–11). However, although alcohol was a normal part of daily life, Old Testament kings and rulers were strongly advised not to drink (Proverbs 31:4–7; Isaiah 56:10–12); and, in the New Testament, Paul advises Timothy that church leaders shouldn't drink too much (1 Timothy 3:8). Why do you think this is?

The Bible contains many examples of harmful conse-quences of drinking alcohol: Genesis 19:32–33 describes how Lot unknowingly commits incest while he is drunk; Esther 1:7–12 and 7:2 shows how the Persian king's moods and decisions are dangerously influenced by alcohol; and Ephesians 5:18 warns, 'Don't drink too much wine. That cheapens your life. Drink the Spirit of God, huge draughts of him.' Notice in this last example that God is giving us an alternative. He isn't depriving us of fun: he's offering some-thing better!

Why do you think drinking 'huge draughts' of the Spirit is given as the alternative to getting drunk? It suggests that there's a link between the two. Sometimes being filled with the Spirit makes people behave as though they're drunk, for example at Pentecost (Acts 2). Or it may be that to drink the Spirit is to taste the absolute best in life, and getting drunk offers nothing in comparison.

If alcohol becomes a fulfilment in itself, then Christians have definitely sold themselves short. We will find better 'solu-tions' for life's problems when we look for them in God.

'The joy you have given me is more than they will ever have with all their corn and wine' (Psalm 4:7, *Good News Bible*). Alcohol makes you feel good, but if there's something lacking in your life, press on after God. He can fill you with greater joy than booze can (and what he gives you will last!).

The Bible seems to say that drinking alcohol is okay as long as it doesn't affect your behaviour and decisions. However, some people think that the sort of wine they had for everyday use in Bible times had a very low alcohol content, and this is why it was all right to drink it. Others feel that although drinking alcohol was acceptable in Bible days, it is less so now because it can do so much more harm, eg through traffic accidents. What do you think?

Addiction

It's pretty obvious that God wouldn't want us to be addicted to anything. Addiction interferes with people's relationship with him and robs them of their potential. The Bible says it's like slavery (Titus 2:3). The good news is, Jesus came to set slaves free!

The Bible also makes clear how much God hates idolatry: this is where a person's dignity, values and relationships are sacrificed to a false 'god'. Addiction is a form of idolatry, because the 'god' is the thing the person is addicted to. God values self-control, and someone who is addicted has lost control over a particular area of his or her life.

People often ask if addiction is a sin. That's a tricky one! In many cases, addiction is more like the consequence of sin: 'The one who sows to please his sinful nature, from that nature will reap destruction...' (Galatians 6:8, *NIV*). Addiction is the 'destruction' that someone reaps from repeatedly giving in to self-indulgent desires.

How we can decide

According to 1 Peter 2:13–15 we're to live within the law so that we set a good example and others can't use our behaviour as an excuse not to think seriously about God. This answers any questions about whether we should use illegal drugs!

What about substances that are legal, like tobacco, solvents and Poppers? What if other drugs were made legal one day – would it be okay to take them then? This is where we have to bear in mind the wider context in which we make decisions. Let's look at some of the principles we can draw from the Bible to help us decide.

THE BODY

The body is made and sustained by God, so we should take good care of it (Genesis 2:7). Anything that abuses the body abuses God's handiwork and insults him. If we are Christians, the Holy Spirit lives within us (Ephesians 2:22). Do we really want to abuse the place where God lives? If we have given our lives to God, even our bodies belong to him – they're not our property to do whatever we want with (1 Corinthians 6:19–20). This principle can be applied to things like food, sex, driving our cars too fast...

GOD'S RULES

Why does God give us rules? What motivates him? When parents say to their children, 'Don't stick your finger in the light socket', or 'Don't eat all those sweets', it's not because they want to be mean and deprive their children of something enjoyable. They say things like this to protect their children. Parents are more aware of the possible consequences of an action than their children are. Even if a child throws a tantrum, the loving parent will still say, 'No.' It's the same with God. He gives us rules and asks us to stick to them because he can foresee the harmful consequences of not doing so, while we can't (Deuteronomy 4:40).

Sometimes God gives us rules to make sure we get the very best out of life (Psalm 19:7–11). A survey found that 3 out of 5 couples who had sex with each other before they were married now wish they had waited. They have discovered that doing things differently from what God, our designer and loving parent, intended meant that they got second best.

When we ask, 'Is this wrong?', what we usually mean is 'Will I get into trouble?' Once you understand God's motivation, a better question would be 'Is this what he thinks is the best thing to do? If not, why not?'

THE DEVIL

The devil's plan is to rob, kill and destroy us. He wants to take away the satisfaction that can only come from going for God. (Sometimes he doesn't have to take it away from us – we offer it to him!) He gets pleasure from things that degrade and humiliate people, that rob them of the dignity God has given them. He loves destroying lives.

Unfortunately, the devil is the best con-man ever. He is the father of lies (John 8:44), and can come to us disguised as an angel of light (2 Corinthians 11:14–15). He robs us by tempting us with things that are so attractive they look better than what God is offering. The devil often fakes God's gifts. For example, by filling us with the Spirit God gives us REAL joy: we know that our lives are safe in his hands; we can feel peaceful and free from anxiety and fear. Being drunk with alcohol is the devil's counterfeit of this. He tries to convince us that this kind of feeling is 'the real thing'. But he's lying. It's only a superficial 'happiness', a short-term relief from anxiety or pressure.

The devil gets us to forget that God always wants the best for us. He has been trying to do this right from the start. God told Adam and Eve that they could eat fruit from every tree except one. They had so much choice – all they needed for a lifetime of variety. But the devil immediately focused on the one thing God said they couldn't have, because it would harm them, and he made them feel they were being deprived. Adam and Eve's downfall came because they doubted God's word and stopped relying on him alone.

The devil still does this. God has given us enough 'Yes's for a lifetime of fulfilment, but the devil draws our attention to the few things God has said we can't have or do because they will damage us. The devil tells us, 'It won't do you any harm. Don't let God deprive you of something good.'

Whether we're talking about drugs, smoking, how we spend our money or use our leisure time, the way to measure the value of something is to ask ourselves, 'Does it improve or destroy? Will it help us to realise our highest potential? Or will it rob us?'

God's grace

Have you ever done something you shouldn't, thinking 'God will forgive me, so I may as well do it.' I have! When we think like this, it means that we have forgotten what God's motives are. We have fallen for the lie that other things can satisfy us more than he can, or the lie that he is depriving us of something worth having. We have also drastically undervalued his love and overlooked the effect of sin on us, on God and on other people. Imagine agreeing to marry your wonderful boyfriend/girlfriend and then saying, 'But I want to spend the weekend with my ex. Please let me know how much I can get away with without blowing it completely.' Playing around with God's grace is a bit like doing that.

God's grace allows us to sin but, far better than that, it allows us to choose not to sin. If God forgives us the things we do wrong, isn't this even more reason to please him and to use our freedom in a way that honours him?

CONSIDERATION AND CONSCIENCE

In his letters written to the church in the first century, Paul provides guidelines to help the Christians decide if they should eat meat that has been used in idol-worship. Although he is talking about food, we could insert 'smoking' or 'alcohol', or drugs if they are legal. Paul gives two major principles to guide us in our decision making. Can you spot them here?

'All food is clean, but it is wrong for a man to eat anything that causes someone else to stumble. It is better not to eat meat or drink wine or to do anything else that will cause your brother to fall … But the man who has doubts is condemned if he eats, because his eating is not from faith; and everything that does not come from faith is sin.' *(Romans 14:20–23, NIV)*

'God doesn't grade us on our diet … But God *does* care when you use your freedom carelessly in a way that leads a Christian still vulnerable to those old associations to be thrown off track.

'For instance, say you flaunt your freedom by going to a banquet thrown in honour of idols, where the main course is meat sacrificed to idols. Isn't there great danger if someone still struggling over this issue, someone who looks up to you as knowledgeable and mature, sees you go into that banquet? The danger is that he will become terribly confused – maybe even to the point of getting mixed up himself in what his conscience tells him is wrong.

'Christ gave up his life for that person. Wouldn't you at least be willing to give up going to dinner for him – because, as you say, it doesn't really make any difference?' *(1 Corinthians 8:9–13, The Message)*

If we are Christians, we are part of one body, the church, and the actions of one person will affect others. And this is true even if we don't belong to a church. God values relationships above everything else. He doesn't want us to make decisions as though we were the only person on the planet, thinking only about what's good or fun for us.

Can you think of situations where you might apply the principle of not doing something because it could throw someone else off track?

These verses from the Bible also say that while in God's eyes something may not be 'wrong', if our conscience tells us not to do it and we do it anyway, it becomes wrong. This may sound a bit tight, but remember – God is interested in what's going on in our hearts. If our conscience tells us something is wrong but we do it anyway, what does that say about how much we value him?

FREEDOM

Jesus has set us free from legalism, that is, from always having to be on our best behaviour to try and keep in God's good books. But this freedom brings responsibilities:

'Do not use your freedom to indulge the sinful nature; rather, serve one another in love.' *(Galatians 5:13, NIV)*

'Live as free men, but do not use your freedom as a cover-up for evil; live as servants of God.' *(1 Peter 2:16, NIV)*

SELF-CONTROL

God values self-control because he is self-controlled (2 Timothy 1:7; 2 Peter 1:6). He wants us to control our desires rather than be controlled by them. This will give us more time and energy to invest in other people and other things. We will be better able to take on responsibility. And we will generally feel more positive about ourselves.

In street culture, lots of things end up back to front. For example, being out of control on alcohol is seen as being mature, and violence is regarded as 'manly'. But this is a lie. God wants us to value and respect ourselves and other people, because we are all made in his image (Genesis 1:27).

SPIRITUAL HEALTH

Remember — we are body, soul and spirit. Things that appear to affect only one area often affect them all. Drug use has a spiritual dimension, not just a physical and emotional one. In my experience, there can be a link between abusing drugs and leaving yourself open to demonic oppression. The will acts as a door, choosing what we let into our minds, emotions and spirits, and what we keep out. Under the influence of the drugs, the will is sedated, and it's as if the door is left wide open. Because you're doing something God says we shouldn't do, you're inviting spiritual problems.

I know this sounds heavy, but most Christian ex-drug users (from all denominations!) tell me they have needed ministry to be released from demonic oppression. You need to be aware of the full extent of what you could be letting yourself in for.

8 THE REAL HIGH LIFE
Why we are here

In chapter five, we saw that we all need to feel significant. If we don't know why we're here, we will wander through life – having some interesting experiences along the way, perhaps – but never finding real satisfaction.

Live to give

The truth is, we exist for God – to have a relationship with him, to love and serve him. Our society's 'consumer' mentality may cause us to think that WE are centre-stage and that everything, including God, exists to make our lives more enjoyable. But the reality is that the eternal plot of the universe revolves around Jesus: we only become significant because God has decided to involve us in that plot. Jesus said:

> 'This is how much God loved the world: He gave his Son, his one and only Son. And this is why: so that no one need be destroyed; by believing in him, anyone can have a whole and lasting life. God didn't go to all the trouble of sending his Son merely to point an accusing finger, telling the world how bad it was. He came to help, to put the world right again.' *(John 3:16–17, The Message)*

It's when we take part in God's plan to 'put the world right' that we find our true purpose. When Jesus called Simon and

Andrew (Matthew 4:18–20), they left behind their whole way of life to follow him. They were willing to make this huge change because he was offering them something far more satisfying than they had ever experienced before. What do you think would have happened if they'd told him, 'We'll give you one day a week, but that's all we can manage'?

After loving God, the second reason for living is to 'love your neighbour as yourself' (Leviticus 19:18). But how do we 'love our neighbour'? We're all pretty selfish really, aren't we? Yes, but we're designed so that, like Jesus, we get our greatest fulfilment from having our deep needs met by God, then letting what we receive from him flow out to others. Selfishness is pointless because, in fact, the more we give, the more alive we will be!

WORLD CHANGERS

We usually think that influence comes from having lots of money, power or fame. If you're fifteen, broke and no one wants to go out with you, who's going to notice you?

Every one of us can have an impact on the people around us. Many of Jesus' disciples were regarded as uneducated nobodies by the society they lived in, yet he showed them they could influence the whole world through who they were, by their attitudes and lifestyle (see Matthew 5 – 7).

Take a good look, friends, at who you were when you got called into this life. I don't see many of 'the brightest and the best' among you, not many influential, not many from high-society families. Isn't it obvious that God deliberately chose men and women that the culture overlooks and exploits and abuses, chose these 'nobodies' to expose the hollow pretensions of the 'somebodies'? *(1 Corinthians 1:26–29, The Message)*

Have you ever wondered why Jesus came when he did? If he had come today, he could have contacted millions of people, beaming into virtually every house in the world via satellite and cable TV, and the Internet.

And why did he live the way he did? If all he had to do was die for our sin, why didn't he live a life of luxury before letting himself be executed when his time was up? I think it's because helping people to know God isn't just about passing on information: Jesus wanted to show people PERSONALLY what God is like. He did preach to crowds, but a lot of his time was spent dealing with individuals in depth.

Today Jesus does this through us. Many of the structures in Western society, eg the legal and education systems, were built on Christian values. But some of these values are in danger of being lost in our present 'anything goes' culture. We need to show individual people within the less-than-ideal realities of life what God is like, so that their lives and these structures can be transformed. Sometimes I feel that the problems of society are too big for me. Yet I CAN make a difference right now to the lives of a few people at least. In chapter nine the stories of Andy and Neil demonstrate the kind of impact we can have on people around us.

Often when people are young, they have big dreams. But because their dream seems impossible, or doesn't happen as quickly as they expect, they talk themselves out of it. Some dreams are just part of being young, but some are God-given. Imagine Mary being told she was going to have a baby even though she was a virgin ((Luke 1:26–38) – you can't get more impossible than that! But Mary didn't say to the angel, 'Don't be stupid!' Instead, her answer was a scared but excited 'Yes' to being part of God's purpose. I know it must be easier to believe your life-calling if it's explained to you by an angel, but do you get the point? The

Bible is full of ordinary people through whom God did extraordinary things.

HISTORY MAKERS

Recently, I've felt God drawing my attention to how William Wilberforce transformed the society of his day by getting Parliament to abolish slavery. How did he do this, and could anything like it be done now? It took twenty years of campaigning to get slavery banned. We too must be willing to persevere if we want to see big changes happening in our society.

Second, abolition wasn't a one-man show – it happened because a team of people all worked together, using whatever gifts they had, whatever influence, to bring about their goal.

Finally, and most importantly, at the height of their campaign they prayed for three hours a day! This sounds totally tedious, doesn't it? But God wants us to be gripped by the desires of his heart. When we are, we get caught up in the excitement of prayer, and become more and more aware of its potential to change people and situations. Often when God is preparing to do something big, getting people to pray is the first step. Remember, everything flows from our relationship with him. If we spend time with God in prayer, we'll long for the things he longs for. The Holy Spirit will be changing us on the inside, so we'll know when and how to take action.

You're not 'on hold' until you're an adult: you have a part to play right now. We are living in a very significant time. Many young people are anxious about the future. But ultimately the whole universe is under God's control. We don't need to feel weighed down or afraid.

In the Bible, Paul compared the Christian life to running a race (1 Corinthians 9:24–25). Imagine this is a relay race. Throughout history, each generation has run its stretch of the course before passing the baton on to those on the next stretch. Soon the baton will be passed to you.

Within the last forty years or so, through the renewing work of the Holy Spirit, a whole generation of Christians has rediscovered a freshness and relevance in the language and style of worship, and more people are taking an active part in church life. But it mustn't stop there. The Holy Spirit is far bigger than our 'small', church-focused ideas. The challenge that faces us is the world 'out there'. God has given us the Holy Spirit to help us in the task he has assigned to us, that of letting the whole world know how much he loves us and what Jesus did for us. But this will only be fulfilled when we take this task out of the church and into society, and go beyond words to living out his message.

When Jesus was teaching his disciples how to be history makers and world changers, he told them that those who followed him should have the same effect on the world around them as salt and light do (Matthew 5:13–16). Salt stops food from going bad and prevents it from tasting bland. Light cuts through darkness, exposing where danger lies and showing people the way, so they don't stumble around or fall. What use is salt that stays in the salt-pot, or a light that's hidden under the bed? We are a very significant part of the answer to our society's problems.

I'd like to end with a psalm – Psalm 24, which was written to celebrate the return to Jerusalem of the Ark of the Lord's Presence. This psalm could be an anthem for our generation.

Psalm 24

The earth is the Lord's, and everything in it.
  The world, and all who live in it;
for he founded it upon the seas
  and established it upon the waters.

Who may ascend the hill of the Lord?
  Who may stand in his Holy Place?
He who has clean hands and a pure heart,
  who does not lift up his soul to an idol
  or swear by what is false.
He will receive blessing from the Lord
  and vindication from God his Saviour.
Such is the generation of those who seek him
  who seek your face, O God of Jacob.

Lift up your heads, O you gates;
  be lifted up, you ancient doors,
  that the King of glory may come in.
Who is this King of glory?
  The Lord strong and mighty,
  the Lord mighty in battle.
Lift up your heads, O you gates;
  lift them up, you ancient doors,
  that the King of Glory may come in.
Who is he, this King of Glory?
  The Lord Almighty –
  he is the King of glory.

The material and human world was made by God and belongs to him. There must be a relationship between the Creator and those he created.

To know God intimately, we must aim to be the people he wants us to be, both in how we behave and in our attitudes. This means not looking to our 'idols' (ie things other than God) to satisfy our deep needs, nor building our lives on the lie that we can manage without him.

When we know God intimately, everything good we could ever need will follow.

God is looking for a generation of people who will want to know him like this. He wants them to look to him rather than just to what he does for them. They will discover that he is a God who can transform even a weak, manipulative man like Jacob into someone with dignity and vision.

Doors that have been closed for centuries will then be opened, and God will come into the world, into our lives, in glory.

He will come in strength and power, to claim what is rightfully his. All those who want to know him will be ready to open those doors for him.

So let's do it!

9 SORTED
Helping someone with a drug problem

One of the most heartbreaking things the family and friends of a drug user have to face is the realisation that there's little anyone can do to get that person to stop. As you will have seen from the true-life stories in this book, people take drugs as long as they seem to have something to offer. Many won't give up until the pain outweighs the pleasure. The best thing you can do, therefore, is to stop protecting drug users you know from the consequences of using drugs, so that they reach the stage where they've had enough.

How 'hurting' can be helping

First, let's look at how we can stop protecting people from the consequences of their drug use. This sounds very cruel. Is it really necessary? According to the Bible 'A friend loves at all times' and 'There is a friend who sticks closer than a brother' (Proverbs 17:17; 18:24). Friendship involves loyalty and commitment. But how does this fit with not protecting someone from the consequences of using drugs? 'Wounds from a friend can be trusted' (Proverbs 27:6). Part of being committed and loyal may mean 'wounding' someone. If your friend is doing something that will harm her, isn't it kinder to say or do something before it's too late, even if it hurts her feelings? Loving someone means doing what's truly best for that person, not burying your head in the sand.

How 'helping' can be hurting

We are probably all guilty of trying to help in ways that actually give people the green light to go on doing something that's wrong or harmful. This is called 'enabling'. For example, if your brother finds maths difficult and you do his homework for him, it may seem like a great idea because he keeps out of trouble and you are owed a favour. But if it means he never learns to do maths, have you really helped?

We do things like this because we want to be liked and accepted. Sometimes we really believe that what we're doing is right, but a lot of the time we're actually stopping others experiencing the consequences of their choices. As a result, they carry on making unwise decisions. As children we learn that being a good friend means covering up for your mates to keep them out of trouble. But true friendship involves caring enough to help someone face the reality of their situation. On pages 116–118 is a scenario showing what hurting, not helping, can look like. What were the various people in the story actually doing for Dave? What could each of them have done differently, and how might it have affected him?

Here's a list of the most common ways we help people to carry on abusing drugs or alcohol. Which can you spot in the picture story?

> Pretend it isn't happening
> Make excuses
> Blame other people
> Blame yourself
> Make it seem less serious than it really is
> Avoid talking about it
> Try to control the user's behaviour
> Join in

NEXT DAY.

WHAT WERE YOU PLAYING AT SATURDAY NIGHT? YOU COULD HAVE KILLED SOMEONE!

SHAME IT WASN'T YOU. LIGHTEN UP WILL YOU?!

WHY DO YOU KEEP GIVING HIM SUCH A HARD TIME? WE WERE ONLY HAVING A LAUGH!

NO MATTER HOW HARD I TRY, HE'S STILL NOT CHANGING. IT'S SO FRUSTRATING. MAYBE HE'S RIGHT. MAYBE I AM MORE LIKE HIS MUM THAN HIS GIRLFRIEND.

MAYBE I SHOULD JUST NOT SAY ANYTHING...

HOW TO STOP YOURSELF ENABLING

If you do find yourself enabling someone who is abusing drugs or alcohol, then you are actually part of the problem. For example, if a friend asks to stay the night so her parents don't find out she's drunk, the main issue is whether this happens regularly. If it's the first time, it would be a bit drastic to tell her 'Tough!' But if it has become a frequent occurrence, you could be contributing to a bigger problem if you let her stay. You can refuse to go along without grassing someone up. I know even that can feel cruel, but how can people decide if something is a good idea or not if they never experience the consequences of it?

You'll only truly be helping when you free the user to take more responsibility for herself. This makes for stronger friendships in the long run. However, watch what's going on in your heart. When you decide not to enable someone, are you doing it because you think, *She deserves everything she gets*, or because you love her and want the best for her? You could take the same course of action either way, but you may need to ask God to help you sort out your motives!

Refusing to enable someone isn't the same as being a grass or a kill-joy. You need to work out when covering up might be contributing to a bigger problem, and when it doesn't really matter. Sometimes leaving people to take the consequences of their actions would be completely over the top.

Refusing to enable can be very uncomfortable. It could mean being ridiculed or rejected. For your friend, it could mean getting into an awful lot of trouble! If she does get caught out, you will probably feel that you have done the wrong thing. Often things get worse before they start to get better. But your friend will have to start taking responsibility and facing her problems more honestly. She may then decide to stop what she's doing.

Sometimes it will seem as though you alone won't make any difference. If you don't lend a friend the money for drugs, plenty of other people will, so you may as well give yourself an easier life by going along! But remember:

⚓ Even if there are plenty of people 'out there' who will carry on enabling your friend, it's those who are closest to her who will have the most impact.

⚓ Friendship is a two-way thing. If your friend is starting to use you and putting drugs before your friendship, getting tougher won't threaten the friendship – the drugs are already ruining it.

Here are some steps you can take to stop enabling:

℮ Get honest with yourself and with your friend. Tell her how her drug use is affecting both of you. Do this in a caring and not a blaming way, explaining exactly why you're concerned. Give concrete examples of the things that are worrying you.

℮ Stop accepting responsibility for your friend's problems. Don't try to solve or cover them up. If she isn't held responsible for her own actions, she won't mature.

℮ Take care of yourself, or you won't be able to help others. You need friends to talk to, and to keep going to God for his strength and perspective. The person you're trying to help needs God more than she needs you, so keep pointing her in his direction too.

It's a lot easier if all the people involved with the user can give each other support.

How can we *really* help?

As well as refusing to protect someone who is using drugs, you need to keep on inviting him to do other things. He will probably refuse, preferring to be with his fellow users, but regular invitations will help keep a door open and let him know that he's still welcome in your group of friends. Be approachable and non-judgemental. Be a good listener. Don't take out your frustrations on him!

Jesus was described as 'a friend of sinners'. He hung around with people who weren't regarded as particularly respectable by the rest of society; but they felt accepted by him and comfortable in his company. Yet when he felt God prompting him to take action, he did so. We should aim to be like that – to treat people according to their worth as human beings, whether they're royalty or the homeless on the street, even though we may not approve of what they're doing. We need to pray for others, and occasionally we may sense God prompting us to do or say something to them.

It's important to remember that there are different stages in the development of a drug or alcohol problem, and each requires a different level of response. Don't treat someone who's only taking drugs now and then as though he's got a massive problem. This will just annoy him and encourage him to mix only with other users.

If a friend asks you for help, you may need to involve an older person. Look for someone you both trust and can talk to easily, and if possible go to see him together so that your friend doesn't feel anything's going on behind his back.

What should you do when your friend says he wants to tell you something on condition you keep it a secret? The problem with promising in advance is that once you know a secret, you may feel that you HAVE to tell someone else. What you have heard may upset you, or you may not know how you can help. However, if you do tell someone, your friend will probably never trust you again.

If you think you're about to be told something serious, say from the outset that you can't promise to keep the secret in case you don't know how to help. If you do need to involve someone else, your friend can help you decide who to approach and go with you, so that he stays fully in touch with what's happening. That way your friend still feels safe and in control of the situation.

Andy
●●●●●●

In chapter four, Andy told us what happened to him at the point when he decided he had to sort his life out. For the first time, he had borrowed money – for drugs – off his mum. To him, this felt terrible. Then, after starting a new job that was very important to him, he wrote his car off in an accident.

When I crashed my car, I thought, *If God exists, this is him giving me a chance to sort my life out.* I'd just started working for Neil who had told me at the interview that he was a Christian and he wanted his business to serve God. I was impressed that he was so committed to what he believed in, when everyone around me didn't have a clue what they were doing with their lives.

I could relate to Neil easily – we had similar ideas and ambitions. But it looked like he would achieve his and I wouldn't because of the way I was living! During the years I was taking drugs, I'd never had any guidance from anyone and needed a kick up the backside – so it came as a relief to meet him.

Neil invited me to stay with him while I didn't have a car so that I could still get to work. When I moved in, it was like Christianity came to me instead of remaining something distant. Neil talked to me all the time about what God was doing in his life, and because I trusted him I listened. I started reading the Bible, and found that it gave answers to the problems I was facing. I saw the struggles Neil was still going through, but this didn't put me off. Instead it made me trust him because I saw that he was for real. I finally gave my life to God one night after telling Neil absolutely everything about myself, all my 'darkest secrets'. It was as though the full extent of what I was doing hit me for the first time. I felt I had no other option!

After that, life got much better. But the temptation to do all the old things became a real battle. When my dad lent me a car, I was able to go back to where I'd been living before. I tried then to live with a foot in both camps – I wanted to sort my life out, but I also wanted to keep on taking drugs! Obviously this was totally impossible, but it took me a while to accept it. My thinking was still way off. Like one time, I was really craving drugs, so I prayed and said to God, 'If you want me to have them, make sure the dealer is in.' Then I took the fact that he was as a sign that it was okay to carry on! I eventually realised that to break free I would have to move away from where I was living and distance myself away from old friends and influences until I was strong enough to handle them.

The thing that helped me most to integrate into the church was knowing that I had something to offer. Other Christians need me as much as I need them.

It's sad that churches tend not to offer people who aren't Christians the opportunity to relate to those who are in a way that's real. Christianity was only made relevant to me by my relationship with Neil outside church.

People won't just come into church off the street, and they won't feel it's got anything to offer unless there are activities going on which allow them to interrelate with others. Christians need to build friendships outside the church so that people outside can discover God in the context of those relationships. Once the Holy Spirit works in them, and they've seen that they can relate to Christians in normal life, they'll see that we've got something they need and they'll come to church.

Neil

I knew that I needed to be realistic about the fact that Andy would use drugs regardless of anything I said. Because we were spending so much time together, we got to know each other very well and could be open about things. We would discuss our lives, our dreams and aspirations. Soon it felt very natural for Andy to start talking about God.

Andy could see that my life wasn't all bright and wonderful, and that I was going through a lot of struggles. This was key, because he could see that I was a real person who did real things and who had real problems – in fact, I was the same as he was. It meant that he didn't have idealistic expectations of what being a Christian was about. He could see that Christianity isn't just for people who go to church on Sunday, who earn over £15,000 a year and who have nice homes. I stressed to Andy that it would be challenging to be a Christian. Life would be much happier, but it would be a harder life to live.

I could tell if Andy had been taking drugs, so I used to find a way of bringing it into the conversation. Like he would turn up on Monday morning looking the worse for wear. I'd ask, 'How was your weekend?' 'Fine.' 'Who did you see down the pub?'... And so it would go on, and we'd just chat about his life. It was important that we talked about drugs openly. He could be open because I didn't say, 'You shouldn't do that.' I did talk about the negative effects, not on him but in my own experience. This made it easier for him to talk about how drugs were affecting him. He could say, 'It gets me like that too.' He didn't need me to tell him he shouldn't be doing it – he already knew that!

After Andy had been living with me for a couple of months, I felt that our rapport was strong enough for me to say things more directly. By then he was also concerned about the effect drugs were having on him, and wanted to talk it over with me. He would ask things like, 'How can you tell I've been using Speed?' I told him that I saw how it affected his moods. He found this difficult at times. Sometimes he'd withdraw; other times he'd talk. After a while our friendship was strong enough for me to feel comfortable saying things I knew he'd withdraw from, but which we could talk about later. It's very hard to reach that stage of openness because people usually block it, and if they block it you can't force your way in.

I often asked if he felt I was getting on his case, and let him know that he could tell me to shut up if he wanted to. It's important not to put people under too much pressure, or you end up wrecking the friendship. After all, God gives *us* the freedom to back off or not listen to him! Only a tiny amount of time was spent talking about the negatives of drug use. Andy knew his lifestyle was no good, so we didn't need to focus on it. What he needed to know was 'How do you change all that?'

We used to talk about Christianity all the time. It was Andy who initiated most of the conversations. He could see the life I was living, and he wanted to know more. He would ask questions about who God was, how to pray, what the Bible was. By the time he moved out three months later, he had moved on considerably. But because he went back to his old environment, he went back to drugs. I tried to reassure him all the time, saying that any condemnation he might be feeling didn't come from God. Once he grasped this, he was able to start work on getting himself to the right place with God.

One day he asked me directly, 'How can I get out of this situation?' By then he believed in the Bible, so I could answer directly from it. I told him that the Bible tells us we should remove ourselves from temptation, so he should not only move out of his current lodgings but also avoid living with *any* drug user. Andy desperately wanted to go on with God, but he still needed a push to make a decision and some gentle steering in the right direction. Prayer was important. As soon as he started working for me, I started praying for him, and so did other people.

Analysing it like this makes it sound really hard work, but at the time it felt totally natural. There was no 'battle plan': it just happened. The most important thing is to be real with people, because they know it when you're not. Remember, too, that you can't do it for them. Some people aren't ready to respond to God, but Andy was – and if someone is ready, it will all happen very easily and naturally.

Speeding on

There are four things we need to do.

1 Know God. Everything else follows on from this. 'People who know their God will be strong and take action' (Daniel 11:32). When we know God has called us to do something, we'll be able to persevere. Remember, none of this is about 'being nice'. We can't love God, let alone other people, unless we're receiving his love for us. As we spend time with him and let him meet our three deep needs, he will shine through us to others, showing himself in us.

2 Pray for God's will to be done and his kingdom to come where you live. In the end, it's only the Holy Spirit working in people's hearts which draws them to God. Although we should try to live a lifestyle that reflects what God is like, this isn't all there is to it. Lots of people knew Jesus and still chose not to follow him. If HIS life and teaching wasn't enough to convince them, ours certainly won't be!

3 Sort out your life. Aim to be a positive role model. We must think big, pray big while remembering that God wants us to make a difference to the people around us right now. In order to change the world,

we have to be changed! While we aim for that, remember that God will use us even though we're far from perfect. Some of the people whose stories are in this book became Christians through the influence of other Christians who still had problems in their lives. For example, Rebecca heard about Jesus again from someone who was still taking hard drugs!

✝ Do what God tells you to do. This is about US joining HIM in carrying out HIS plans.

When Jesus was on earth, the last thing he said was this:

'All authority in heaven and on earth has been given to me. Therefore go and make disciples of all nations, baptising them in the name of the Father and of the Son and of the Holy Spirit, and teaching them to obey everything I have commanded you. And surely I am with you always, to the very end of the age.' *(Matthew 28:18–20, NIV)*

This is the task we're meant to be getting on with. Generations of Christians ahead of you have run their stage of the race. Now the baton is about to be passed to you. What is God wanting to do in Britain and in the world during your life-time?

Even while you're waiting for your turn to run, you're a vital member of the team. Cheer on those who are running ahead of you. Learn from them. Copy and improve on what they got right. Ask God to show you how to do differently the things they're getting wrong.

You will only have one go at your stage of the race, so be ready. Be responsible with the task God has given you. When the baton is passed, hold on tight – and go for it!